CAPE MAY COUNTY
and the
CIVIL WAR

CAPE MAY COUNTY
and the
CIVIL WAR

RAY REBMANN

THE
History
PRESS

Published by The History Press
Charleston, SC
www.historypress.com

Copyright © 2025 by Raymond Rebmann

All rights reserved

First published 2025

Manufactured in the United States

ISBN 9781467158657

Library of Congress Control Number: 2024947366

CONTENTS

PREFACE

W hile New Jersey was considered by many to be a "border state," having pro-Southern leanings in the coming split in the Union, parts of the state remained steadfastly loyal to the North, especially after the commencement of hostilities. Cape May County, isolated and sparsely populated, was one such region, surprising given the county's close economic connections with the South, the especially nationally known seaside resort Cape Island, which attracted many affluent southern visitors in antebellum years.

And while not many men called the county home (total population around seven thousand), those who did so rallied to the cause, enlisting in the state's infantry and cavalry regiments. Most of the Cape May County men fought in the battles of the eastern armies at places previously unknown to them with names like Fredericksburg, Chancellorsville and Gettysburg.

Some died from bullets or disease or exposure to the elements. Some were wounded. More survived and came home to a county that was undergoing dramatic changes as modern technology in transportation and communication opened sleepy Cape May County to the rest of the world.

This book tells the stories of these men who fought in the Civil War. It describes how that war affected and changed people at home and describes how people responded to both a prolonged and bloody conflict and to changes that eventually transformed the county from an aggregation of agricultural communities to the major travel destination it is today.

Cape Island sketch around 1862. Note the lighthouse. *www.geographicus.com*.

I do not go deeply into the "big" names of the Civil War. This is not a story about the strategies of Grant and Lee. Their stories have been told extensively elsewhere. I only describe battles of that conflict that involved men from Cape May County.

I spent hours reading books, examining personal journals, newspapers and letters. More hours were spent poring over documents and records at local museums and libraries. While the goal sometimes seemed elusive, I could not have persevered to complete it without the support of my wife, Alicia.

I was also fortunate to have access to materials at the Old School House Museum in Dennisville. Additionally, the Cape May County Library has preserved most of the *Ocean Wave* newspapers of the era. Those papers served as an essential background for this effort.

Last but not least, the work was helped by a generous grant from the New Jersey Historical Commission Department of State and Cape May County Board of County Commissioners through the Cape May County Division of Culture & Heritage.

CAPE ISLAND

W hat else can be so grand at night when the hall is cleared of tables and hundreds of gas jets are brilliantly burning and flickering and the gay and elite are flushed with the giddy dance," as a guest described Congress Hall in the 1850s. "Then you behold a scene, beautiful and fair."

Newspapers celebrated Cape Island for its "seaside entertainment…its sea bathing, extensive rooms, its fish, oyster and crabs, its good liquors….All at the beautiful confluence of Delaware Bay and the ocean," as noted one, the *Daily Aurora*.

Cape Island considered itself prim and proper, instituting strict protocols for beach use, according to Harry Weiss's *Life of Early New Jersey*. "Ladies at appointed hours of the afternoon may go into the surf at which time, gentlemen do NOT walk on the banks." Mansion House, operated by R.S. Ludlam and William S. Hooper, established its own system: "A white flag will be on the bath houses during the ladies' hours. A red flag for the gentlemen," according to Weiss.

By mid-century, Cape Island had become America's favorite seaside resort. President Franklin Pierce visited in 1855, arriving over Fourth of July weekend at the urging of Secretary of War Jefferson Davis, another seasonal visitor. Steamships from Philadelphia stopped at New Castle, Delaware, collecting well-to-do southern passengers visiting Cape Island. Another line ran regular service from New York with stopovers at Cape Island before steaming to Philadelphia.

Captain Wilmon Whildin's *George Washington* made three weekly trips to Philadelphia, while a half dozen steamers traveling the New York–Philadelphia route visited the resort. Whildin added two steamers between Philadelphia and New York and installed a wharf near Cape Island.

Visitors brought their handsome horses and carriages to show off along the Promenade. During evenings, they filled the ballroom at Congress Hall, dancing to the music of Hassler's Band from Philadelphia, the "best orchestra on the coast," as noted in the *Cape May Ocean Wave*.

Guests enjoyed duck hunting, bracing saltwater plunges and spring water drinks from "famous" Cold Spring before enjoying the pleasures of the evening. Southern gamblers frequented the Blue Pig, a noted hot spot. It wasn't uncommon for gentlemen to wager entire plantations on the turn of a card. The "Pig" was a "select" house, operated by the North's "most famous gambler," Harry Cleveland, but it wasn't the only game in town. Another gambling establishment was a three-story affair. Black servants waited on white patrons while sporting gents from the South mingled and gambled with the North's "racy set." All night long, young people drank and danced and set off fireworks. Business boomed, and men like Jeremiah Mecray and James Miller became rich.

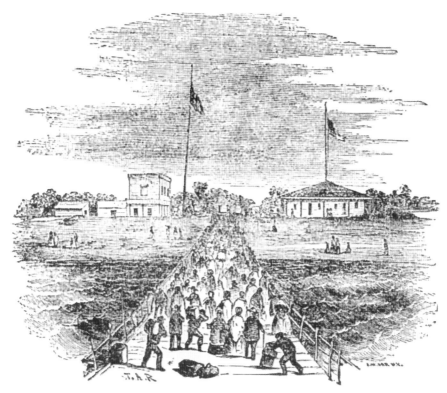

Opposite: Congress Hall in the nineteenth century, still operational as of 2023. *www. caperesorts.com.*

Above: Whildin's steamboat landing at Cape May Point in 1859. *From* Cape May Magazine.

Right: Today's Blue Pig Tavern, located at Congress Hall—not open for gambling. *www. caperesorts.com.*

Cape Island boasted twenty-four hotels, accommodating nearly six thousand guests, according to historian Robert Alexander. Construction thrived as builders scrambled to build seasonal cottages and boardinghouses to accommodate tourists.

President Pierce's successor, James Buchanan, visited to "escape the bad vapors" of Washington. The fastidious Buchanan, a bachelor and known epicure, stayed at Congress Hall, where his niece, Harriet, was installed as official hostess.

But Cape Island experienced setbacks. Fires damaged the resort in 1855 and '56. Two of the island's larger hotels, the Mount Vernon and Mansion House, were destroyed. Room capacity was reduced by half. Another event occurred during these years presaging an end to Cape Island's preeminence when a new resort was born to the north: Atlantic City. In 1854, this rival enjoyed an immediate boost with the introduction of something Cape Island lacked: railroad connections to the outside world. Atlantic City clearly affected Cape Island's volume of trade, but equally significant was the diminished traffic from the South, attributable to the country's worsening political climate.

The county's business interests, having considerable tourism and shipping connections to the South, did not relish the threatened dissolution of the Union that appeared inevitable with the election of Abraham Lincoln. *Ocean Wave* publisher Joseph Leach voiced concerns that a split be avoided because it would hurt business.

Tourism operators still hoped for the 1860 season—"A large number of cottage families are expected and the steamers will commence their trips," according to the *Cape May Ocean Wave*. Instead, Cape Island businesses saw numbers drop by 80 percent. The economy suffered in other ways. Commodities previously obtained from the South became more costly. In her diary, Amelia Hand noted that "wool rose from $.25 to $1.50 a pound, cotton seven cents to $1 and tea forty cents to $1.50."

There was some sympathy for the South beyond the loss of visitors from Dixie. While many residents opposed slavery, they expressed little desire to turn loose "four million Negroes upon the country…a much greater evil." Community groups voiced opposition to "meddling in the domestic affairs of our southern brethren." Rapprochement was their favored solution.

As early as December 1859, meetings were held supporting the Union. Gathering at Cape Island, Colonel John West, Joseph Leach, Richard Ludlam, Dr. James Mecray, George Smith, S.R. Magonagle and others passed a resolution declaring "devotion to the Union of states and

Constitution." They "[a]lso affirmed that the Fugitive Slave Act should be upheld and enforced so that sister states may enjoy all rights and privileges we hold sacred and inviolable." The group supported citizen rights to "carry their property into the territories in submission to the decrees of the Supreme Court."

A newspaper ad emphasized pro-Union sentiment: "No North, No South, No East, No West…Our whole Union…Irrespective of part… condemn all fanaticism."

Following the turbulent Democratic convention on April 23, the *Ocean Wave* noted that "hot-blooded southerners bolted and organized their own convention." "Nevertheless," the paper predicted, "secession will prove a fizzle." Cape Island reflected those growing tensions. Pro-Union Whigs mixed with secession-minded southern Democrats. Heated arguments ensued. At the close of the 1850s, political debates became more strident.

A prosperous era ended with Lincoln's election. A Cape Island visitor in 1860 wrote, "The streets are barren, weeds have taken over lawns, picket fences crumble in the blazing sun."

After Fort Sumter was attacked, Joseph Leach editorialized the necessity of maintaining the Union through military preparedness. But County Freeholders, reluctant to spend money to train and equip volunteers for that preparedness, initially "set aside" requests from John West, captain of Cape Island Home Guards, seeking an "appropriation to help the guards purchase supplies."

"Why should Cape May stand in the rear?" Leach criticized. "Our homes are more exposed to invasion than any others on the seaboard.…Nearly every county in the state has appropriated money for home war purposes." With Washington only one hundred miles away, countians reacted. Committees of vigilance formed. Home militias like the Cape Island Home Guard enlisted volunteers and drilled on the grounds of resort hotels. Militias formed in Tuckahoe and Court House. Dennis Township citizens organized an "independent company." Twenty men stepped forward, enlisting on the spot. Dennis Township men drilled under Joshua Townsend, veteran of the War of 1812.

Over Fourth of July weekend, Cape Home Guard assembled to fire a salute. An otherwise quiet Fourth, the holiday's highlight was an open invitation to partake at Guardsman George Smith's ice cream saloon. Home Guard colonel Charles Powell presided over the election of officers: William Smith (captain), George Smith (first lieutenant) and Richard Tindall (second lieutenant). The Guards' endeavor to raise an entire county company

Dennisville Inn, frequent gathering place for that community, as it appeared before being moved to Cold Spring Village. *Dennis Township Old School House Museum.*

proved unsuccessful, but its members were resolved to fight. By summer's end, they were boarding a steamer bound for Trenton to enlist in a company there. One volunteer was ice cream impresario Smith, destined to become an officer in the 7th Regiment New Jersey Infantry.

Patriotic displays, parades, flag raisings and speeches proliferated across the county. In Dennis Township, a rally was held at Ludlam School. Former freeholder Abraham Reeves, whose family would contribute four sons to the Union cause, spoke at Cold Spring along with Leach and Reverend Moses Williamson. There were flag raisings at Goshen and Fishing Creek. Green Creek hosted another, attended by the ubiquitous Reverend Williamson and Leach, accompanied by the Cold Spring Guards. Afterward, the "ladies of Green Creek provided a bountiful repast," Leach reported.

Patriotism was fully displayed in South Dennis, its schoolhouse "jammed with those devoted to our cause," Leach reported. Outside, Union enthusiasts fired cannons and muskets. After patriotic songs and prayers from Reverend Jesse Diverty, the flag was paraded around the building, "encircling and protecting the youths of the neighborhood." Rio Grande burned Jefferson Davis in effigy during an "Indian clambake as the flag floated in the moonlight atop a 70-foot pole," the local paper reported. It continued, noting that

Davis, "black-hearted traitor, deserves to be driven forth from mankind to live among the hyenas, tigers, and venomous reptiles," all agreed.

The county seat outdid them all. More than one thousand Patriots gathered for the county's "official celebration of the 4th." Union Guards performed military drills, while, according to the paper, the courthouse bell pealed out during a procession of "many of the Court House boys in uniform"to a hallowed place known as "the grove." Speakers waiting to address the throng included Thomas Beesley Esq., S.R. Magonagle and J.H. Diverty. They orated, read the Constitution and issued resolutions supporting the Union.

Businesses embraced the spirit of patriotic fervor. William Townsend's store at Cape Island offered "secession neckties"—"Made of stout hemp rope and so arranged to slip over a person's head....If Jeff Davis were on our shore, the Cape Island Home Guards would present the black-hearted traitor with one, ply it around his neck, and fasten an end to the highest limb of the nearest tree," the *Wave* story concluded.

7TH Regiment

Enlistment in New Jersey's initial four three-month regiments expired following the debacle at Bull Run. Realizing that the war would last longer than early optimistic assessments, the government called for more volunteers, including ten three-year regiments from New Jersey and eight infantry units, along with cavalry and artillery units. The 7th Infantry was one of these.

The *Ocean Wave*'s September 12 edition reported the formation of its Company A. "For the first time in its [the county's] history, so large a number departed for war....On Thursday morning, carriages met at the Armory, Cape Island, and conveyed this gallant set of men, and their families, to the steamboat landing." From there, they traveled to Trenton.

The paper listed twenty-one volunteers in Captain Louis Francine's company. Two weeks later, the paper reported another twenty countians joining the regiment. "The county is doing pretty well considering the population." George Smith penned details about the regiment's arrival in "Dixie": "After a ride of 36 hours in old cars, propelled by a slow engine, we arrived in Washington and sought the 'soft side of a plank' and slept at the rate of ten knots per hour."

The next morning, "knapsacks and muskets shouldered," they headed to Fort Casey. Hot and tired, according to Smith, the men were greeted by a banner, presented by the "ladies of Cape May" and "planted it upon the land of Dixie."

Company A, containing most of the Cape May County men, was led by Francine, the youngest company commander at age twenty-four. Francine possessed a storied background. He'd studied the art of warfare at École Polytechnique, an officer's training school in Paris. George Smith described Francine as a "gentleman and a scholar"—"Our boys are in perfect love with him and will follow him through thick and thin."

Born in Philadelphia, Francine spent his childhood in Camden, attended military school on Long Island and then journeyed to France, where he received his "polishing touches" at the French equivalent of West Point. When war broke out in America, he returned to southern New Jersey and helped raise Company A. Francine quickly impressed superior officers and drew admiration from subordinates. General William Sewell, one of Francine's commanding officers, later wrote in tribute that Francine "was initially a soldier. His gallantry at Chancellorsville was repeated at Gettysburg where he held his regiment under the most terrible storm."

Company A consisted of ninety noncommissioned officers and privates, including thirty-nine Cape May militiamen. George Smith, who'd led that militia, was appointed first sergeant for the company. Fellow Caper Richard Tindall was elected second sergeant. Smith was a man of many talents, including builder and house painter. The 1860 census listed his occupation as "ice creamer." He was also apparently a skilled organizer of men. Like with other New Jersey regiments heading off to war, the 7th traveled by train. Their route was from Trenton to Camden. Next came a short ferry ride across the Delaware to Philadelphia, followed by another train journey across eastern Pennsylvania. Then came a second ferry ride across the Susquehanna, reaching Havre de Grace, Maryland. After a third train switch at Baltimore, the regiment arrived at Washington, where it started learning the fundamentals of soldiering.

Back home, *Cape May Ocean Wave* reported on the progress of the local heroes. The November 14, 1861 edition noted that "the Cape May boys were under arms, wheeling, filing, flanking, marching, and turning...all double quick."

While thus occupied, the regiment welcomed a new officer. John Howard Willetts, a medical doctor from Cape May Court House, had attended West Point. He failed to complete the course, but he learned about tactics and was recommended for a commission. He was assigned captain of Company H.

Second Sergeant Richard "Buddie" Tindall, not yet twenty, was the first Cape May County enlistee to die for the Union cause, but he didn't die in combat. Like many young men away from home for the first time, Tindall succumbed to illness.

The October 17 *Ocean Wave* provided a lengthy obituary. Tindall was the nephew of Richard Swain Thompson (later an officer in the 12th New Jersey Volunteer Infantry). Tindall's middle name was Thompson, after his uncle. Tindall's mother, Mary Elizabeth, Thompson's sister, was the widow of Reverend Napoleon Tindall, first pastor of the 1st Baptist Church of Cape Island. He died in 1855. Mary remarried Samuel Magonagle, who later became publisher of the newspaper.

John Howard Willetts, originally from Cape May County, practiced medicine in Cumberland County. *Dennis Township Old School House Museum.*

When news reached Cape Island about the bombing of Fort Sumter, Tindall was among the first to enlist. He was described as "warm-hearted and genial, quiet and unassuming and firm in his purpose." "His young heart was fired with a patriotic zeal for the defense of the flag…eager to join up after hearing about the attack on Fort Sumter."

Tindall developed high fever from exposure shortly after the 7th reached Washington. Although he seemed to recover and wanted to rejoin his comrades, he subsequently developed typhoid. On the day Tindall died, his mother was in Dennisville, attending a funeral. That night, she left for Washington, where Richard was hospitalized. She learned in transit that he'd died. Magonagle, Richard's stepfather, accompanied Tindall's grandfather Richard Thompson in bringing Tindall from Washington to Philadelphia. His coffin was draped with the flag, presented to the regiment by the ladies of Cape May. He was buried at Baptist Cemetery in Court House.

"The deceased was the first of our gallant sons of Cape May who has fallen a victim to the present war, not by the sword of our rebel enemy but by the still more fatal ravages of diseases induced by exposures and hardships of those unaccustomed to camp life," the *Wave* obituary continued. Tindall had recently married Annie Mecray of Cape Island. Her brother John served with him in the 7th.

The paper published a camp letter from the 7th describing the regiment's reaction to Tindall's death: "We paid him the respect usually paid commissioned officers." The entire company formed with "arms reversed"

WILLIAM S. HOOPER.

Artist's rendering of William S. Hooper, oldest enlistee from Cape Island in 7th Regiment. *www.findagrave.com.*

to escort Tindall's coffin to the train station while the regimental band played the "Dead March." William S. Hooper, John Stites, Walter Barrows and Levi Johnson composed a commemorative resolution honoring Tindall. It praised the late sergeant for "discharging himself faithfully until his dying day."

The 7th embarked on its first operation on November 3 to eastern Maryland. There it supervised elections in that contested state, with voters deciding whether Maryland would remain in the Union. While the regiment encountered no difficulties, the area voted decidedly pro-secession.

The regiment's return to camp was marked by an outbreak of illness. Six men died. Others were bedridden within a month. The paper published a letter from George Smith describing the regiment's "hard time of it, compelled to march sixteen miles a day through ankle-deep mud, with loads of 25 pounds each." That weight didn't include tents. As a result, "thirty gave out and three died from fatigue."

The men became proficient at drilling, especially Cape May's boys in Company A. But in the spring of 1862, they would see real action. Granville Leach reported on those "Cape May boys" from Meridien Hill for the November 14 paper. The first local he encountered, John Stites, was writing a letter, while the rest of the regiment drilled nearby, "under arms, wheeling, filing, flanking, marching and turning all in 'double quick.'"

Leach observed practice loading and firing. Company A was the first to perform. "Instantly, eighty muskets spoke out as if one man fired them at once." The drill was repeated, the men loading and firing as quickly as possible. Once drill concluded, the men clustered around Leach, clamoring for news from home. "Every man had increased in weight," Leach observed, "from five to 20 pounds." George Smith drew special notice, having "grown so large he will soon need a horse as he will not be able to walk or run… and so with his brother [James]….Sheriff [William] Hooper is another upon whom change in climate has begun a great change."

Leach attributed the men's robust "perfect condition" to daily drilling, rain or shine. Leach praised the food: "bread made from the best wheat flour while the soup features rice and beef and plenty of it." He had fewer kind words for their clothing ("scant and deficient for cold weather") and living accommodations ("bed on the ground, sometimes a blanket between them and bare earth").

Leach encountered one "healthy smiling man" whom he recalled as a "pale young fellow" back home, Joseph Johnson.

Private Thomas Fletcher Jacobs wrote about the 7th's movement away from Camp Casey. "We left in heavy marching order carrying our 'bed and board', clothing, and 40 rounds of cartridges."

The regiment reached Georgetown and loaded belongings aboard the steamer *Richmond*. The following morning, the densely crowded transport headed down the Potomac, camping on the Maryland shore, thirty-three miles south of Washington. Men built log huts, uncertain how long they'd enjoy their use. Jacobs estimated Union strength at fifty thousand men. Jacobs also described a new oddity in camp, a "large balloon, which ascends several times a day to view the rebels." Enemy batteries on the Virginia side of the river fired at it without success. Jacobs mentioned that Company A helped move it closer to shore—"Townsend Ireland aided in holding it down as it was moved."

He also noted how close opposing armies were encamped. "We can go down to the shore and hallo over to the rebels but can seldom understand one another." "The boys are well," Jacobs concluded, "and are anxious to meet the enemy."

Jacobs wrote about adjustments to camp life. "They take their India rubber blanket and lay it down anywhere and placing their woolen one over it can stand about any kind of weather." Jacobs's stay with the regiment was brief. According to Stryker's *Record of New Jersey Civil War Soldiers*, Jacobs was discharged in August 1862 due to disability.

The 7th eventually joined the 5th, 6th and 8th Regiments, composing the 2nd New Jersey Brigade, assigned to Hooker's division, stationed on the lower Potomac. The regiment camped across the river from a Rebel battery. The *Ocean Wave* shared another "camp letter" describing that scene: "Thirty-five miles below Washington, camped opposite the rebels. Occasionally, they send us their compliments in the shape of shot and shell and our battery, as gentlemen should, return the compliment."

The letter writer was impressed by Hooker, "a real military man, about five feet ten inches, well proportioned, quick piercing eyes." Hooker was equally impressed by the 7th, calling it a "model company." Their objective was the Confederate force at Manassas. But the Rebels evacuated before the Federals moved. Ordered to Fort Monroe, the regiment left behind several

Union soldiers work with a newfangled spy gadget. *www.battlefields.org*

men, dead from illness. These included John Shaw and John Workman from Company A. Neither had fired a shot in actual combat.

Another casualty from the county, succumbing to disease in late 1862, was Stephen Pierson. Son of David Pierson, trustee of Cape Island Methodist Church, Stephen was eighteen when he was sent home. He died on November 18 from "disease contracted while fighting the battles of his country," as his tombstone at Cold Spring Cemetery reads.

George Smith wrote a poetic New Year's letter for the January 16 *Ocean Wave*. He predicted that the Potomac River would become as historically renowned as Caesar's Rubicon. "Traitorous foes lurked on every bluff and hid behind every thicket, daily and nightly the river shrieks of their murderous shells." Smith described and praised the role of pickets in the

Federal army, "entrusted with the lives of thousands, the picket while his comrades sleep, paces up and down gazing steadfastly upon the river....His duties are simple but dangerous. The lurking hidden foe is ever on the alert and often in the silent watches of the night, the crack of his rifle tells of the life blood draining from the lonely picket's breast...all is reported quiet the next day—only a private shot."

Smith's flowery prose also saluted the arrival of a new year. "It was my duty to pass New Year's Eve on the beach. All was silent save the plashing of the waves as they kissed the pebbles on the shore and receded back into the bottom of the Potomac." The forest "waved in the night wind." Stars "twinkled, seeming to whisper words of comfort to those in so much trouble here below." "'Twelve o'clock and all is well,' went the sentry's cry...the 'knell of the old year."

Another camp letter followed a week later, bemoaning a holiday season passed away from loved ones, "no delightful sleigh rides over crisp fallen snow....How vividly those recollections of happy days rose up before the wind....We are engaged in a civil war and it is for this reason that we are away from home...we will preserve our country and our flag."

Smith detailed some "pleasures" of the soldier's life, like the excitement whenever Rebel batteries lobbed shot and shell their way—"Whizzing of the bomb coming closer and nearer to us." Another diversion was the increasing numbers of deserters from enemy ranks. "Whole regiments would desert if they could," he assured readers.

The 7th joined its division near Yorktown. There the army formed a line across the peninsula. From this position, Union forces laid siege to Yorktown. During this operation, the 7th encountered something that became a faithful and dogged companion during its stay in Virginia: mud! They slogged through it, got stuck in it, camped in it and ate and slept in mud. And they worked in it, digging trenches and building fortifications. Worst of all, many men became sick in it.

A "private" letter from Joseph Johnson included a pencil drawing of the camp, including the twenty-by-forty-foot-log cabin "our boys occupy." The paper shared Johnson's description of the cabin: "The roof is made of straw. The cabin is divided into two 'apartments', each room warmed by an oven built of stone and clay....The men sleep in bunks...four to a bunk." The regiment toiled on a "log road," while Leach repeated the soldier's common lament: "impassable," rain-soaked roads.

The Johnnies pulled out of Yorktown, moving toward Richmond. The 7th was ordered forward in pursuit during a downpour that turned those roads to soup. The Rebels reformed at Fort Magruder about five miles from Williamsburg. In spite of darkness, the difficulty of travel along mud-washed roads and bone-tiredness after the long march, the regiment anticipated engaging the enemy. The next day, their wish was granted: an attack on Fort Magruder...in the rain.

Confusion settled among elements of the Union army assaulting this position. At one point, the 7th advanced, entering woods. Holding the far left of the Federal line, the men loaded their muskets, not easy given the wet conditions. Company A advanced, and the enemy fell back to a line of felled trees and rifle pits. After the Federals fired, the Rebels counterattacked. Francine ordered his company to retreat, leaving several wounded. Enemy attackers swelled in number. "Bull Run!" the Rebels shouted, intending to demoralize their foes as they pursued their retreating adversary.

The 7th had to contend with numerous enemy tricks—Rebs pretending to be Union soldiers, Johnnies carrying white flags or flags bearing Union colors on one side, Confederate stars and bars on the other. This time, the 7th moved out of the woods into adjoining fields, encountering men waving a national flag and identifying themselves as "Pennsylvania boys." The Union men held fire. The enemy opened up, creating casualties among the inexperienced Northerners.

The 7th finally repulsed their attack, scrounging among dead and wounded for ammo once their supply was exhausted. During a lull, the Confederates reinforced. They charged through the woods in three brigades. The 7th wavered. Men went down, killed or wounded. Weapons became fouled in the wet weather, and panic set in as the Rebels attacked on the front and flank.

The Union line was finally reinforced and the attack beaten back. But the Rebels launched another, which the 7th met with a ragged volley. Some units broke to the rear, while others stayed, bearing the brunt of the assault. The regiment gave way grudgingly, and their resistance prevented a rout of their division.

"New Jersey may well be proud of her sons in this battle," the *Philadelphia Inquirer* reported. "The conflict at Williamsburg proves that the Jersey Blues of our day are worthy descendants of the heroes of the revolution." "Following the occupation of Yorktown," noted the *Ocean Wave* in February, "the 7th joined the pursuit of the fleeing enemy," catching up with them after a soggy nine-hour march over the usual muddy roads. "Terrible was the slaughter on both sides...til nearly nightfall," the paper reported.

Francine shared details in the *Wave*'s next edition. "Having marched for hours in a downpour, men camped in the woods without any shelter but trees." They carried sixty rounds of ammunition, further weighing down knapsacks as they moved through "knee-deep mud." Exiting the woods near Williamsburg, "the spires of the town rise to view."

"Directly in front of the road is situated the strongest of the rebel entrenchments." The 7th was third in order of attack against this defense.

Company A deployed as skirmishers. They were immediately fired upon, losing four dead, two wounded. The Cape May boys were indeed "seeing the elephant." Division commander Joseph Hooker was more succinct: "There's no doubt in my mind that the New Jersey troops would fight." And they would die. Twenty-eight men were killed, with another eighty-six wounded. Among these were several men from the county. Three were hit at the same time. Locals Townsend Ireland and John Mecray were killed— "news of their death has spread gloom over this community." Two other locals, Stephen Bennett and Charles Silver, were wounded.

Mecray, from Cape Island, was hit in the head with a shell fragment and killed instantly on May 5, 1862. Son of Jeremiah Mecray, one of Cape Island's wealthiest men, Mecray would be memorialized on the island when GAR Post 40 was named for him after the war.

Private Stephen Decatur Bennett was wounded in the left leg, between the knee and hip. The bullet passed through his body, lodging in his haversack. He managed to crawl over to Ireland, who'd been hit by three bullets. Ireland rolled onto his back, gasping. "Oh Lord, I am gone."

An officer later found Bennett still alive and had him carried off to have his wound dressed. Ireland died as the line threatened to collapse before reinforcements surged forward, driving the Rebels back. "Townshend Ireland lay near John Mecray where they fell about the same time," the May 15 *Ocean Wave* reported.

Afterward, a long trench was dug, and the dead were interred side by side. The names of those sharing the common grave were written on papers placed opposite the bodies after the trenches were filled. The 7th lost thirty-nine killed.

Bennett was sent home to Cape Island. He told the local paper about his combat experience while he struggled to recuperate. "Company A was first to open fire and gave as good as they received until the rebels were reinforced and were trying to flank and it was folly for our men to hold their position so they fell back contesting every inch of the field."

Bennett and his comrades contested their advance. "Our young hero was firing from behind a tree, 'picking off his man' as three rebels advanced towards him." When they were within sixteen paces, he fired. The Rebel he shot "kicked up his heels, keeled over, and died."

Reinforcements relieved beleaguered defenders, enabling an orderly retreat. Bennett was left lying with Mecray and Ireland. Rebels emerged from concealment to search the fallen dead and wounded. "They took Ireland's and Mecray's money and asked Bennett if he had a pistol. They then ransacked his pockets and took sixty cents."

Bennett was taken prisoner. His wound bleeding profusely, he was dragged over a mile before his captors abandoned him for dead. The next morning, he was found by Union soldiers and sent to a hospital in Philadelphia. His mother retrieved him there and brought him home on a steamer, his wound still bleeding during the journey.

A week later, the paper reported Bennett's death at home on May 27. It also published an unconfirmed report that another local, Charles Silver, had also died. Granville Leach followed up with a report from Fairfax, Virginia. "The boys from Company A raised some money to send home to Ireland's widow." The amount was $76.50, not an insignificant sum for the time.

The paper's lead column that week featured a tribute to another Williamsburg casualty, Charles Silver. Wounded in action, Silver succumbed and was buried at Fort Monroe. "Suspense is past—anxiety's o'er—The warrior's dead—he fights no more."

Silver hailed from Heislerville but walked from there to Cape Island to enlist with the Cape May boys along with his friend Fletcher Jacobs. "When on the island, he told us [the newspaper] he wished to be considered a 'Cape May soldier.'"

Directly beneath that tribute, the *Wave* ran an article discussing the fate of "American Negroes." "Where shall they be colonized?" "Send them to Liberia. Or Haiti." "Colonize them in one of the southern states." The article wasn't by-lined, but the author indicated his preference for colonizing in the South rather than "exporting the problem."

He cited cost as one factor. Another was white "guilt." The writer suggested that it would be a "sin" to force people to remove to a foreign land. "In any event, it would be cheaper to send them south. And poetic justice too." The writer even offered picks for colonies, primarily South Carolina, birthplace of the secession. Choice number two? Texas. "Nothing but a headache since begging to be admitted to the Union."

Levi Johnson, a private in Company A, was discharged in July 1862. Ironically, Johnson's discharge resulted when he was injured while tending the wounded. Illness and non-combat injuries resulted in more discharges than combat wounds. Exposure to the elements in that swampy area was a major factor, disabling even Cape May County boys who grew up near swamps.

Due to numerous losses, primarily illness-related, the regiment fielded a fraction of its original strength. And having no officers fit for duty, Company A command devolved to First Sergeant George Smith. Performing picket duty while awaiting further orders, the regiment experienced another change among officers. Captain Willetts was promoted to lieutenant colonel and reassigned to the recently formed 12ᵗʰ Regiment.

Lee's Army of Northern Virginia continued moving, driving the Federals south of Chickahominy River. Retreating Union forces settled at Harrison's Landing on the James River. "When we arrived," Smith wrote to the *Ocean Wave*, "we were almost starved having but three days rations during the whole time we were fighting."

As top-ranking member of the regiment, Smith approached the quartermaster to procure rations for his men. "Imagine our disappointment when the quartermaster informed me, he could not honor my requisition unless it was signed by a commissioned officer."

When Smith explained the 7ᵗʰ's personnel predicament, the quartermaster adamantly insisted on the "rules." Even in the midst of war's carnage and deprivation, a bureaucrat remains a bureaucrat. Smith eventually dogged an officer, had his paperwork "properly" authorized and fed his hungry men.

Smith's predicament was resolved when Francine, recovered from his illness, rejoined the regiment, but Smith was officially made an officer as well, promoted to second lieutenant. Smith's promotion was duly praised by his hometown paper, which noted that the new lieutenant "received a sword worth $35 with an inscription showing the sword had been presented by his captain, Louis Francine." Fellow countians Joseph Johnson and Charles Weeks were promoted to corporals, rewards for "meritorious conduct at the battle of Williamsburg."

In sadder news, the paper reported that Isaac Hall and Edward Filkins were sick in a Philadelphia hospital. Both would be discharged for medical reasons.

As the year ended, the regiment welcomed a special visitor when President Lincoln reviewed the troops. "President Lincoln rode along our brigade and reined in his big black stallion," Smith wrote. "He looked up and down the ranks and there was hardly a man with a whole pair of trousers or blouse." Many of the soldiers were shoeless. Smith thought they looked more like an "army of tramps than soldiers." "[T]ears chased down his [Lincoln's] cheeks. He pulled off his great silk hat, bowed, rasping in a choking voice, 'God bless you boys' and rode on....Never was there a greater, more touching speech made during the war." The men turned away, many shyly wiping away their own tears. The incident, according to Smith, filled the men with "fresh determination to stand by the old flag."

So ended the Peninsula Campaign for the Cape May County boys. The *Ocean Wave* July 10 edition featured more correspondence from Smith, writing from camp at Fair Oaks following the Battle of Williamsburg. Smith demonstrated considerable facility with the pen in his communications with his hometown paper, which was perhaps disposed to publishing his writing since the peacetime "ice creamer" maintained regular advertisements in the *Wave* for his Cape Island business. While Smith dished out righteous retribution against his country's "traitors," Mrs. Smith was home, dishing out scoops of vanilla and chocolate at their Ice Cream Saloon and Confectionery Store on Washington Street.

In this correspondence, Smith took umbrage with a Philadelphia newspaper's suggestion that Union troops, especially New Jersey's, were proving less than valorous in battle. "It seems hard for the New York and Philadelphia correspondents to give the Jersey Blues their due," Smith retorted. "We've had a lively time here…almost daily, rebels throwing shells or making attacks on our pickets…the most cowardly thing a soldier can be guilty of."

Smith described an enemy sortie that was repulsed several times before they withdrew "with heavy losses." "I think they will get tired of this kind of fun for they always get the worst of the bargain," he wrote. Attrition took a toll on both sides. According to Smith, the 2nd Brigade, originally four thousand strong, was down to two thousand "effectives." "We all think the general should bring up some other brigade to relieve us as there are many in the rear doing nothing." No doubt he would have included certain Philadelphia newspapermen in that category. Having served with the regiment since the start, Smith was well placed to judge morale. "The boys are getting along first rate and are ready to meet the rebels at any moment." They'd soon have their chance. John Reeves wrote from camp "near Williamsburg" on May 8. Assuring readers that he was "alive and well," Reeves shared impressions of the recent battle, observing that "we had 60 rounds of cartridges besides the 40 we always carry in our cartridge boxes."

Captain George Smith. *Avalon Historical Society.*

Men fell behind during their recent march, according to Reeves, an "effect of the dysentery" on the regiment. When the battle line finally formed, "only 82 men were in place." Reeves also decried the weapon he was compelled to use. As "bullets flew all around us…our old smooth bore muskets got so stopped up with powder we had to put our ramrods against a tree and drive the cartridge in that way."

Fighting finally stopped at night. "We were soaking wet, had nothing to eat…we couldn't find our knapsacks so we had not a blanket…but managed to get a fire…a most wretched night but daylight came at last." Unfortunately, the enemy located those missing knapsacks and helped themselves to their contents. They also looted the dead from both sides, including the bodies of Townsend Ireland and John Mecray. "All of them had been robbed… Townsend had $15. He'd sent $10 to his mother and was going to send the rest as soon as he received her answer to his letter.…Poor fellow, he will never get an answer."

Reeves experienced a close call when enemy cannon fire struck two comrades near where he and fellow countian Ike Hall were marching. The shell "took one man's legs off and the arm off another and their screams made us feel bad.…But after we got into the fight, I was just as cool as though firing blank cartridges on drill."

Reeves added that the wounded would be sent to Philadelphia, although he doubted that "Steve" Bennett would make it, while the boys from Company A had buried and marked the graves of Ireland and Mecray. Reeves noted that Hall was at the moment "beside me in camp…writing home to his mother."

Back in camp, the 7th was visited by Thomas Hughes, owner of Atlantic Hotel. "That same jolly fellow he was before we left home." His visit reminded them they were only halfway through their three-year enlistment. Toward summer's end, the 7th encountered Stonewall Jackson. In late August, the 7th marched fourteen hot miles before facing enemy lines near Bristow Station. Jackson's army had been wrecking rail lines, destroying a Union supply base at Manassas. The Federals were disappointed to find everything destroyed, especially rations the hungry men had anticipated eating. Instead, they resumed marching, this time to Bull Run.

The following morning, August 26, in a downpour, the 7th engaged Jackson's army with John Pope's Army of Virginia. The 7th was hurled against a well-defended railroad embankment, behind which Confederate troops laid down deadly fire. Company A went out first, exchanging skirmish fire with the defenders until jammed weapons compelled the men to pull back.

Regrouping, the regiment moved to the left, where it was attacked from two sides. The regiment retreated into the woods near its starting position.

Because their supplies had been destroyed by the Rebels, the men returned to camp famished and, for many, shoeless and nearly naked.

The battered 7th remained at Fort Lyons, outside Washington, for the next month, as the army reorganized. Part of the restrengthening effort involved recruiting by active members of the regiment. Sergeant James Smith was dispatched to New Jersey to solicit volunteers. Smith reached Cape Island for that purpose after opening a recruiting office in Newark. Reorganization included top command of the Army of the Potomac. McClellan was out and Major General Ambrose Burnside in.

The *Ocean Wave* published an "anonymous" letter stating that while the 7th largely missed the carnage at Fredericksburg, "[W]e were near enough to rebel balls to have one man killed and two wounded in the regiment.... When Burnside made a second attempt to cross the river, we had our finger in the pie, building a road to extract the artillery from the mud."

Also returning to Cape Island was Corporal William Hooper, home on furlough. One of the oldest members of the regiment, Hooper nonetheless impressed folks at home with his "fine spirits and determination to rejoin his regiment as soon as possible."

Also home, but in much poorer condition, was Stephen Pierson. "He has been sick with typhoid fever followed by chronic diarrhea for more than two months," the *Ocean Wave* reported. He'd been hospitalized at Newark since early September. There he stayed until his father secured his discharge and brought him home. "He is reduced to almost a perfect skeleton and it appeared hardly possible that he'd long survive." The paper optimistically added that after a few days home, Pierson appeared to improve. However, he died on November 18.

After Pierson's funeral, a woman who had lost a son in the war was heard to remark, "You cannot tell until you have experienced the feeling it gives one to see a coffin covered with that flag."

Having received marching orders on November 1, the regiment "marched all day, slept in open fields, with 40 rounds of minie balls for a pillow and broad sky for a cover." No sooner had they snuggled in than they were ordered to Bristow Station, advancing ten miles to Warrenton Junction. With little rest for the weary, they were moved again—back to Bristow Station! There they were greeted with a snowstorm.

Even with snow falling steadily, they weren't permitted to sleep. Marching in darkness so thick they had to "feel their way," they eventually arrived at the very place they'd vacated a day before. The resourceful men quickly threw up "shanties" using wood the Rebels had left when they'd withdrawn. These makeshift structures "appeared like pig sties," but the men didn't care.

The quartermaster eventually procured standard-issue, and far less commodious, tents. Scratch carpentry rendered former "sty" walls into flooring. The 7ᵗʰ settled in, rigging "bake-ovens" to mass-produce bread. They hoped they'd found a home for the winter.

It was not meant to be. Snow covered muddy Virginia when the 7ᵗʰ rejoined the rest of the army at Falmouth. Many men were still poorly equipped, lacking certain essentials like weapons and shoes. Neither shortage was rectified when the regiment slogged forth, barefoot and carrying antiquated muskets that routinely malfunctioned in the heat of battle.

But south they marched. Their ultimate destination was Fredericksburg. Gathered at the Rappahannock River the morning of December 13, the regiment was finally issued rations, three days' worth, along with one hundred rounds of ammunition. They crossed the river on pontoon bridges to meet the gathered Army of Northern Virginia. Lee's men were perfectly positioned, having had time to deploy while Union engineers constructed those pontoons. The 7ᵗʰ, fighting against Jackson's army to the south, was spared the failed assault at Marye's Heights.

Suffering serious casualties after a number of unsuccessful attacks, Burnside ordered retreat. The 7ᵗʰ manned a picket line during this movement. The regiment was the last Union unit on the wrong side of the river, a dangerous situation given that they faced the entire Rebel army alone. Avoiding a slaughter, the regiment crossed just as the pontoons were removed.

A defeated and demoralized Army of the Potomac returned to Falmouth base camp. There it licked its wounds for a month before Burnside again decided to try outflanking Lee.

On the night of January 20, 1863, the 7ᵗʰ Regiment, down to three hundred effectives, left Falmouth. Of course, it was pouring, drenching scantily clad soldiers. Rain persisted the following day, rendering roads so impassable that the regiment was compelled to march through the woods, cutting down trees to create a corduroy road for supply wagons to traverse.

Still the rain came down. The men couldn't build fires because of it. They ate cold rations because of it. They became sick because of it. Conditions became so intolerable that some deserted, figuring that the firing squad was better than what they were enduring. The so-called Mud March took a greater toll on the 7ᵗʰ than had its experience at Fredericksburg.

The fiasco ended with another change in top command. Hapless Burnside was out. Joe Hooker was in. Maybe it was improved food and more of it, or the new uniforms. Perhaps it was the arrival of improved weapons or increased attention given to soldier health. Perhaps it was the furloughs that finally came through. Maybe symbolism played a role…a new regimental flag replacing one thoroughly shot up in combat. Likely, a combination of all these improved morale of the Army of the Potomac under its new commander.

Spring brought sunshine and Fightin' Joe Hooker's first offensive as commander. In early May, the 7th re-crossed the Rappahannock, positioned on the right wing. A portion of the regiment guarded the pontoon bridges while the rest performed reconnaissance detail.

However, the enemy was elsewhere, as was the fighting, with disastrous results for the Union army, which retreated toward Chancellorsville, Jackson's gray coats hot in pursuit. The 7th moved forward to plug a gap in the Federal line toward Chancellorsville. Company A deployed as skirmishers, while the rest of the regiment established behind makeshift breastworks. Company A returned in a hurry, Rebels at its heels.

Firing intensified on their right as the enemy advanced. Francine ordered his men into the woods, where they grouped parallel to a road (Plank Road), facing toward it. From this position, they observed the Rebel advance. Waiting until their targets were closer, the regiment directed several volleys, driving back the enemy. "The enemy hurled brigade after brigade against our position," Francine wrote in his report, "but were repulsed each time with great slaughter."

The 7th fixed bayonets and charged, firing as they advanced until the men routed their foes. They then returned to their position, allowing a second Rebel unit to nearly pass before opening fire into its rear. The surprised Rebels broke. A third Confederate unit, from North Carolina, quickly came up. For the third time, the 7th opened fire, routing them. Amazingly, the 7th suffered no casualties during these encounters.

Francine withdrew the regiment to its original position, giving the men time to clean their weapons, fouled in the heat of combat. As they did so, gunfire in their front grew louder and closer. A Pennsylvania regiment beside the 7th suddenly broke, retreating right through the 7th position.

The 7th formed its line and charged, reaching the line gap before the enemy, taking casualties in the process. In the heat of the action, shouting his orders to be heard, Francine lost his voice.

The battle raged for hours but the Jersey boys held. Colonel William Sewell (of the 5th Regiment) assumed overall command when General Mott was wounded. "By maintaining a flanking position under heavy fire for over three hours, the 7th captured five stands of colors and prisoners, including one colonel, one major, and several line officers," Francine wrote in his official report.

The 7th's contribution to the failed Union effort included "15 distinct charges upon the enemy while taking 500 prisoners," also included losing forty-seven killed or wounded. Among those wounded was newly minted captain George Smith, a bullet through his face. Smith was carried to the rear and left, thought to be dead. The *Ocean Wave*, in a brief report on May 21, informed readers that Smith was hospitalized in Washington. "At first, he was unable to swallow even liquid nutriment except through a tube." Describing the severity of the wound, "breaking" his jaw, the paper noted that "the man who shot him took deliberate aim from only a few feet from him."

Meanwhile, the 7th advanced beyond the woods, volleying into the Rebel flank, taking prisoners while advancing toward Plank Road. Sewell ordered an advance across an open field. The charge succeeded in routing the enemy. Union attackers regrouped near the Chancellor House. Here they were rejoined by Francine, who'd gathered scattered stragglers from the regiment, totaling four hundred men.

"With a rush and a cheer and a storm of bullets, the whole line went in," the *Washington Chronicle* reported. "The Jersey brigade that day won lasting renown." Along with "renown" won, the 7th lost forty-nine men killed or wounded. Hooker ordered the entire army to re-cross the river. His plan had failed.

George Smith was carried off the field by fellow Cape May Countian Swain Reeves. Because the bullet had hit him in the chin, passed through his tongue and then out through his neck, army surgeons felt they could do nothing for him.

Reeves had enlisted as a private along with Smith. In December 1862, Reeves was promoted to corporal. He participated in all the engagements of the 7th Regiment from the Siege of Yorktown to the Siege of Petersburg. He was wounded several times. He would be wounded the first day at Gettysburg by a shell fragment. Later at Petersburg, another shell fragment wound, in the heel, wasn't enough to put him out of action. He returned to his regiment and was

Swain Shaw Reeves in later life. *www.findagrave.com.*

again wounded in the left hip by a Minié shell. The shell apparently did more damage to his canteen than his hip because he remained with the regiment until he was mustered out.

After the war, Reeves returned to his Cape May Point farm, which he developed into a market-garden enterprise. He also served as Cape May coroner and elder in the Presbyterian Church. A display at Cape May County Museum includes a soldier's canteen bearing marks where a bullet struck it—Reeves's canteen. The canteen "may have saved me, as it deflected the bullet that struck me, preventing more serious injury," he noted.

When Reeves returned and learned that doctors had given up on Smith, he placed him in an ambulance and had him taken to a hospital at Falmouth. Even there, Smith was initially set aside as lost, but a female nurse—a rarity in military hospitals at this point in the war—cared for the wounded captain. Surgeons finally set his jaw, and Smith eventually recovered. However, his combat career was over. "The wound did not want to heal," he later wrote. "I couldn't eat hardtack, which is very essential to a soldier in active service."

Smith was not county-born but rather came east from Cincinnati at a young age after the death of his father. With his mother and two brothers, he settled in Philadelphia in 1844, where he learned the house painting trade. In 1850, drawn by work prospects on growing Cape Island, Smith moved there to ply his trade. He became active in business, including at the Cape Island House. He was elected alderman in 1861. War interrupted his political career.

Smith was mustered out of the service as a captain on January 7, 1864. He missed the Battle at Gettysburg, but his brother William did not. Originally a captain in the Cape Island Home Guard, William Smith became second lieutenant with the Pennsylvania 106th infantry. He was killed at Cemetery Ridge.

George Smith returned to Cape Island and was elected to city council. While unable to fight, Smith maintained his military associations. In December 1863, after county freeholders voted $300 bounties to entice enlistments to meet the county's quota of 171 men, Smith was picked by the governor as recruiting officer.

Even during a brief stint as first postmaster for Avalon, a new barrier island community, developing in the postwar era, Smith remained connected with First Methodist Episcopal Church of Cape May, where he was an active member for more than fifty years. Described by local historian Robert Elwell Sr. as a "cheerful and faithful Christian," Smith served as superintendent of its Sunday school.

Throat wound notwithstanding, Smith sang in the choir for thirty years. For many years prior to his death, he suffered as an invalid but still maintained his stalwart position in church and community, according to Elwell. "Tell them I am dead in body but wonderfully alive in spirit"—his last message to fellow congregants, delivered over the telephone, a modern technological wonder that allowed Smith to participate in services from his sickbed. On April 23, 1907, his body was laid to rest.

The 7ᵗʰ remained at Falmouth for a month, recuperating from Chancellorsville. About 350 men reported for duty, all now combat-experienced veterans. On June 11, a rejuvenated regiment was again on the march pursuing the Army of Northern Virginia, as it moved toward Shenandoah Valley. The 2ⁿᵈ Brigade (including the 7ᵗʰ) marched up the Rappahannock toward Orange and Alexandria Railroad.

Once camped, the men enjoyed the luxury of bathing, washing away dust of the past month. Then, following a sampling of fresh coffee, they indulged in some snoozing. The following day, after a long hot hike, the 7ᵗʰ finally reached Manassas. Only 25 of the 250 men who'd set out arrived punctually. The rest straggled along as strength and perseverance permitted.

Meanwhile, Lee moved his army into Pennsylvania. After a night camping on cliffs overlooking the Potomac valley, surely a memorable sight for flatlanders from Cape May County, the brigade crossed that river on June 25, marching along the Ohio and Chesapeake Canal before camping near Monocacy River. Marching through Maryland, the 7ᵗʰ learned that it was working for another new boss, Major General George Meade. Instead of shadowing, Meade planned to engage the enemy, an urgency now that the Confederates had invaded the North. That inevitable clash of armies would soon commence at a location neither commander had chosen.

The 7ᵗʰ was initially assigned to guard Emmitsburg. However, in the early morning of July 1, the regiment was ordered forward to Gettysburg. Upon arrival, the men deployed along a line about a mile long, assigned to support eight artillery batteries, two of which were placed in an orchard. They were subjected to heavy fire, "a terrible storm of shot and shell," while they formed in the Peach Orchard before reaching their assigned station on the lower end of Cemetery Ridge.

A movement by General Daniel Sickles, still subject of animated discussion by Civil War scholars, had advanced his corps closer to the front, his right wing extended along Emmitsburg Road with its center at the Peach Orchard. The regiment formed behind the center of this line, just where

Confederate general James Longstreet intended to attack. Longstreet did so that afternoon. "The enemy had now approached to within 200 yards, yelling and shouting," read an official report.

Moving to higher ground in a rye field, the 7th encountered heavy artillery fire at the Peach Orchard. Francine positioned his men behind a fence, ordering them to lie down while artilleries dueled. Enemy shells landed among the prostrate men. The 7th sustained casualties as the Union position broke down. The artillery units fell back toward Cemetery Ridge. Instead of following, Francine ordered the 7th forward to support the hard-pressed Federal infantry. In the confusion and din of artillery fire, not all the men heard the order. Some advanced, while others remained in place.

Adding to the chaos was the withdrawal of the battery. Horses and caissons tangled and blocked the road, separating units from one another, while Longstreet's men advanced, firing as they came. For three hours, the 7th held against vastly superior numbers, despite taking heavy casualties under an enfilading fire. "The enemy now being on our left flank, Colonel Francine threw the right of the regiment forward and opened fire," the official report stated. "After firing a few rounds, a charge was attempted but the enemy fire was so severe they were compelled to fall back."

The effort appeared "hopeless," according to *New Jersey Troops at Gettysburg*. "All knew that any further advance meant certain annihilation for the brave Jerseymen." Francine struggled to reorganize, waving his sword to rally the men. He fell, shot through the leg. He was carried toward the rear, helped by Cape Islanders William Kirby and Corporal William Hooper.

Forty-four-year William Smith Hooper was one of the oldest enlistees in Company A. Before the war, Hooper was proprietor of Mansion House, owned by his cousin Richard Smith Ludlam. Hooper was elected county sheriff from 1856 to 1859 and held other elected and appointed offices, including tax collector and jury commissioner. One of nine Cape Island men who originally enlisted in Company A to survive their entire enlistment, Hooper experienced more than thirty major engagements, including Chancellorsville, Gettysburg, the Wilderness and Cold Harbor. Ultimately, Hooper's service rendered him an invalid with dysentery. "Cranky and feisty even into old age," his *Evening Telegraph* obituary read, "Hooper lived to be 80 years old, dying August 2, 1896."

The entire corps was now in disarray. Men retreated, regiments broke up and officers struggled to reorganize and rally them. The 7th made it back to Cemetery Ridge and stabilized a defensive position. Many wounded were left behind, presumably to die or be taken prisoner.

July 3 dawned on a weary, much diminished 7ᵗʰ Regiment. Casualties ran high, as did the number of missing soldiers. But stragglers found ways back throughout the morning until there was sufficient manpower to return to Cemetery Ridge. The 7ᵗʰ was not actively engaged in repulsing Pickett's assault that day. However, its share of the previous day's battle had taken a considerable toll—ten officers killed or wounded, along with twenty-two enlisted men dead and another sixty-eight wounded. Of the latter, twenty-four men suffered wounds of such severity as to warrant medical discharge.

Francine succumbed to his wounds on July 16. For his gallantry, he was promoted to brigadier general just before he died. Today, a silent monument in the shape of an iron shell stands in that place. Its simple caption reads, "Colonel Francine fell here."

The *Ocean Wave*'s first edition of 1864 would include a plea from Smith on behalf of disabled William Kirby of Fishing Creek. Smith asked former comrades and the community at large to raise money for Kirby, who lost a leg at Gettysburg. The editor opined that Kirby's case was appropriate to be undertaken by Cape May County Soldier's Aid Society and the Board of Freeholders, noting that the county had been generous with bonus money but had overlooked three-year volunteers who'd joined up without such financial inducement. "Justice and merit demand this favor for Mr. Kirby."

At this point, only seven of the original thirty-nine men who left Cape May County at the start of the regiment's service still remained active as the 7ᵗʰ camped near the Orange and Alexandria Railroad, expecting to move any time.

The spring of 1864 brought more changes, including another new commander: U.S. Grant. The Rebels reached Spotsylvania ahead of the Federals. Once again, the 7ᵗʰ was called on to attack a Rebel position. And once again, its effort fell short. A few men tried to hold their ground, but once panic set in, most headed for the rear. There, men reformed a line, and another attack was attempted. This, too, ended in failure.

Had something happened to the fighting spirit of the 7ᵗʰ Regiment? Many of the men had nearly finished their three-year commitments and had not reenlisted. Perhaps that influenced a reluctance to risk lives. In addition, the regiment included new enlistees who'd received little training before being rushed into combat. The same held true for much of the army.

Nevertheless, Grant was determined to move forward and mount another attack. Heavy rain further dampened the martial ardor of the 7ᵗʰ as it moved into place on the third line of the army's next endeavor. The morning of May 12 dawned in dense fog. The men breakfasted on coffee

7th New Jersey Regiment monument at Gettysburg. *www.civilwarintheeast.com.*

beans (chewed) to stay awake while awaiting orders to move, which came promptly at 4:00 a.m.

The 7th rushed forward, filling a gap in the front line, clambering over Rebel breastworks to capture a battery before the enemy counterattacked, forcing them back into the woods. There the men were packed together so tight that they had no choice but to face the enemy and fight it out. With men close behind reloading and passing guns forward, the regiment maintained a steady fire, suffering casualties but holding their position until late into the night. Finally, the Confederates withdrew.

Grant's army moved again. By the morning of June 2, after an all-night march, they had reached a village with the curious name Cold Harbor. There, seven thousand casualties were amassed in a futile attempt to break Rebel lines. In this conflict, the 7ᵗʰ was held in reserve, spared the carnage.

The relentless Grant next moved against Petersburg, south of the Confederate capital. The enemy reinforced Petersburg, and when the order to attack finally came, they were ready as the 7ᵗʰ moved into place behind two New York regiments. In the ensuing charge, a number of men were hit, including Sergeant James T. Smith, Company A, another brother to George Smith. James's wounds would result in his being mustered out of service in October.

Ten men of the 7ᵗʰ were killed in the battle before the regiment was ordered back to the trenches. The Rebels attacked while the 7ᵗʰ fortified its defensive position. The assault came on both flanks and from the front. Surprised Federals streamed rearward in confusion, with Company A separated from the rest of the regiment. Running in the wrong direction, forty-two were captured, including Thomas Van Winkle, who was confined at Danville, Virginia. Van Winkle would be paroled, looking like a "human skeleton, more dead than alive," after eight months' confinement. However, he would recover and return to Cape May County. He later worked as a crewman at the Cape May Life Saving Station at Cape May Point. He died in 1923 and was buried at Tabernacle Cemetery in Erma.

The 7ᵗʰ was soon down to 231 effectives, officers and men. But Grant's war of attrition stubbornly chipped away at the Army of Northern Virginia. The last official act of the 7ᵗʰ New Jersey was marching in Washington's Grand View victory parade. Its colors waved proudly, listing all the battles the regiment fought from Bull Run on. By the war's end, the regimental flag had become riddled with holes, perhaps more holes than the thirty-four stars. That flag was with them in the parade.

Finally, on July 17, 1865, the Cape May men went home. The flag went with them. In 1907, George Smith donated the flag to the City of Cape May. In 1938, the city donated it to the county museum.

10ᵀᴴ REGIMENT

John Wright was first in a line of Cape May County Wrights to serve in the armed forces, from the Civil War to the Iraqi conflict. Descendant Howard Wright, from South Seaville, in a college paper wrote that "farms and water" played important roles in Wright family history.

John Wright was born in Tuckahoe in 1827. He settled in Joelfield, a place that no longer exists but was once a small community in Upper Township. His enlistment papers showed his occupation as "waterman." He earned his living working the bays around Corsons and Townsends Inlets, catching clams and oysters. After the war, he found a ready market for his products in a new resort: Sea Isle City.

Wright was a patriot. When the call came for men to save the Union, John Wright responded. He joined the 10ᵗʰ Regiment New Jersey as a private on December 31, 1863, assigned to Company K. According to Howard Wright, he was a "litter bearer with the rank of private." As with so many of his comrades, he would be discharged before the war's end—in his case, October 10, 1864, due to disability.

With nine companies of infantry and one of cavalry, the 10ᵗʰ New Jersey Regiment was an anomaly from its inception on October 9, 1861. The mix of foot and horse was one difference. The regiment's creation without consent of the state's governor was another, even though it was known as "Olden's Legion."

William H. Donnelly wrote about his experiences with the 10ᵗʰ in a journal that came into the possession of Charles Tomlin, author of *Cape May Spray*. Excerpts from Donnelly's "reminiscences," at Cape May County Museum, are included with the museum's permission, in this account of the 10th.

"I enlisted October 4 [1861] at the age of 18, in what was supposed to be the 9th New Jersey Regiment," Donnelly recalled. "After being camped at Beverly, we found out there had been men who enlisted as infantry, cavalry, artillery, and also a Zouave company." Uniforms for the misfit regiment were issued by Pennsylvania, and weapons came from Keystone state arsenals.

After Donnelly observed the *real* 9th Regiment at the train station, leaving for Washington, a number of confused enlistees sought out Governor Charles Olden, who, in Donnelly's words, "had nothing to do with us" because of confusion about authorization to form the regiment in the first place. Told that they were an "independent" regiment, some of the men deserted.

Charles Smith Olden, New Jersey governor from 1860 to 1863. Previously he was a state senator. *New Jersey State Museum.*

By the time the regiment had moved to Washington, it was down to 180 men. Most of the deserters returned to the fold after Olden "accepted" the regiment, designating it the 10th. Consisting of 883 noncoms and enlistees and 35 officers, the 10th departed Camp Beverly on December 29, 1861. Once settled in, the men did nothing.

The 10th was held in disdain by "regular" military authorities because of its shaky origins. Lack of organization and discipline among the members didn't enhance its image either. Considerable buck passing ensued between Olden and the War Department to accept the 10th as part of New Jersey's required contribution to the war effort and, in the words of historian John Young Foster, "place it [the regiment] on a proper footing for service." This was apparently accomplished by February 1862.

A large part of the regiment's organizational difficulties was a matter of identity. Was it a cavalry unit or infantry? One company that wanted to ride rather than march joined the regiment "equipped" as cavalry. Arrested for declining to dismount and join their comrades on foot, these men were mustered out and their places refilled. The 10th then *looked* like an infantry unit.

Richard Townsend from Dennis Township was among the original three-year enlistees, mustered in as first sergeant in early October. Townsend would eventually transfer out to the 12th in 1863.

Perhaps the youngest member of Company B was Aaron Moore, who enlisted in 1861. If available records are correct, Aaron was fifteen years old at the time. He not only served his three-year enlistment, but he also reenlisted and served until July 1865. Incidentally, Moore would live to the ripe old age of eighty-three.

His captain in Company B was a Tuckahoe man, Charles Claypool, fifteen years his senior. While still on duty in the capital, James Creamer from Upper Township was discharged on March 5, 1862, due to disability. Creamer's brother Frederick, who was serving at the time in the 25th Infantry, died of typhoid fever in a Philadelphia hospital one year later. Both Creamers are buried at Steelmantown Cemetery in Upper Township. A third Creamer, Reuben, served in the 25th, completing his nine-month enlistment.

The 10th finally went to work in the summer of 1862, performing provost duty in the federal capital. The men hungered to fight, but for the balance of the year, requests to join the Army of the Potomac were denied. The 10th stayed in Washington.

According to Donnelly, who was promoted to sergeant, Company B dressed in "blue uniforms with brass epaulets on the shoulders, 'Company B 10th' on their caps, paper collars and white gloves," all while guarding government offices and performing burial details at the National Home.

Another county man in Company B, Sergeant Stephen Sheldon from Eldora, succumbed to typhoid, coming home to die in Dennisville on August 23, 1862. His brother Francis enlisted as a private a week later in the 25th Infantry. The *Ocean Wave* pressed for volunteers to avoid imposition of a draft. The paper implored veterans to reenlist, holding out the promise of bonus money for those who joined.

Sergeant Harry Lawrence, from Dennisville, penned a "camp correspondence" for the paper in October 1862. Recovering from illness at the time, he reported the regiment's continued presence in Washington, with his Company B on "detached service." Their principal duty? "Guarding hospitals, prisons, government buildings, also to apprehend and confiscate all intoxicating liquors exposed for sale within the city."

Lawrence listed names and hometowns of the men from Cape May County enrolled in the regiment, starting with Captain Charles Claypool from Tuckahoe. Following rank in descending order were First Sergeant Richard Townsend, Dennisville; Second Sergeant Harry Lawrence, Dennisville; Second Corporal Jeremiah Barber, Tuckahoe; and Corporal James Robinson, Tuckahoe. Privates from Dennisville were Elvy Creamer, Mathias Creamer, Jonathan Camp, Aaron Moore, Samuel Morton,

Dennisville Inn as it looks after restoration at Cold Spring Village in Lower Township. *Dennis Township Old School House Museum.*

Tenbrook Price, John S. Robinson, Thomas Towzer and Augustus Lutz. Other county privates were Samuel McCarty, West Creek, Francis Garrison and Robert Thompson, Goshen, and John Beebe, Hendrick Layton, Joseph Layton, Henry Warner and Israel Gifford, Tuckahoe.

Lawrence acknowledged the 10th's initial poor image, blaming it on being "cursed with poor officers." But he assured readers that the problem had been remedied since reaching Washington. He quoted from the *Washington Republican* praising the regiment's performance in the capital, assisting the police: "This regiment has not received the credit from the citizens that it deserves. It is one of the best regiments in the service…in point of discipline, sobriety, and intelligence."

Lawrence mentioned a visit from "Dr. Armstrong," formerly of Dennisville, now serving as surgeon for a New York regiment. Doctors with the Union army kept busy. Typhus hit Company B hard. Thomas Tozer died on January 8, 1863, at age twenty at Kalorama Army Hospital, of "complications" associated with typhus. Shortly after the war, his father received a payment of $22.73, the army's compensation to the family for losing their son.

Robinson died in mid-October 1862, while Lawrence himself eventually received a medical discharge on February 10, 1863. Another Dennisville man, Jonathan Camp, fell victim to smallpox in May 1863. With new staff officers commanding them, the 10th entered Virginia on April 12, 1863, marching to Suffolk, then under attack by Rebels under Longstreet. Suffolk was an important railroad junction at the head of Nansemond River, covering land approaches to Norfolk. Suffolk had been taken early in the war by the Union. The Confederates wanted it back.

Longstreet's force, thirty to forty thousand strong, crossed the river to retake the roads to Norfolk while cutting Union supply lines. The 10th was part of the force positioned to stop them. After Rebel attacks and siege efforts failed, the 10th was sent in pursuit of the withdrawing enemy and suffered its first casualties.

The *Ocean Wave* reported an incident that occurred involving the 10th and the 170th New York, near Suffolk at a location the paper called the "Deserted House." "They were each advancing on a separate road, the two roads converging. Between the two roads was a thick growth of underbrush."

As the two regiments drew closer together, they failed to recognize each other. First one and then the other opened fire, the paper not distinguishing which regiment initiated the action. "Considerable damage" was done, the paper lamented. "We have never heard a definite account of the casualties, but reports say that some 40 were killed and wounded."

A few weeks later, the paper published a letter from Claypool, Company B captain. Claypool's "true statement of the affair" began with the morning of May 15 "just before daybreak." "We [10th] were falling back from Carrsville where we had a recent brush with the enemy," Claypool wrote. "Our object being to keep the rebels off the working party that was tearing up the Seaboard and Roanoke Railroad."

The 10th was in the advance, the New Yorkers following, through an area thickly overgrown and so dark that objects could not be made out at a distance. They were supposedly fired on by "guerrillas." In the ensuing confusion, the 170th commenced firing in "every direction, several balls whistling over our regiment which caused us to think the enemy had attacked in earnest." It didn't last five minutes, Claypool noted. "The whole affair was one of those unavoidable incidents that will sometimes happen and I cannot see where any blame can be attached to either officers or men." Unfortunately, both Union regiments suffered casualties before advancing without further incident.

Instead of remaining with the Army of the Potomac, the 10th was dispatched to Philadelphia on July 1 as a show of force to prevent disturbances during the first draft. "[N]ow stationed in Philadelphia, they [the 10th] came from the Peninsula to assist in repelling the invasion of Pennsylvania but the [draft] riots were quelled by the time the regiment reached Philadelphia."

The 10th missed the carnage at Gettysburg, but fate was not so kind to Richard Townsend. Joining his new regiment as a newly promoted second lieutenant a few days before the 12th engaged at Gettysburg, Townsend was killed during his first action as an officer. Having missed the 10th's earlier baptism of fire at Suffolk, Townsend fought at Gettysburg with no combat experience.

While armies clashed on farm fields to its west, the 10th performed provost chores in Philadelphia, remaining there for two months until moving to Pottstown, Pennsylvania, to monitor potentially riotous coal miners. Companies were detailed to Pottsville and Hazelton.

Others were stationed in Mauch Chunk (Jim Thorpe today), where riots had erupted the previous November. The 10th remained through the winter, establishing military governance of Luzerne, Carbon and Schuylkill Counties. Labor unrest was further aggravated by news of the draft. The miners understood that they'd likely be impacted. "We arrested about 300 people who resisted the draft there and sent them to Fort Mifflin on the Delaware Bay," Donnelly recalled. "These people organized and called themselves 'Buckshots' and later the 'Knights of the Golden Circle.'"

On November 5, 1863, two dozen miners paid an unannounced call on George Smith, a small coal mine owner in the region. It was not a social call. Faces blackened to conceal identities, the men invaded Smith's home. After a brief scuffle during which revolver shots were fired, Smith lay dead, a bullet wound to the head. The men, workers in Smith's mine, returned to their homes—homes owned by Smith's mining company.

That brief tragedy played out in the midst of growing unrest in Pennsylvania's anthracite region. Smith was typical of small mine operators, paying low wages for arduous, dangerous work. Smith had given miners further cause for anger recently by cooperating with local authorities rounding up draftees. Smith provided lists of employee names, including locations of dwellings.

The war never enjoyed much popularity among immigrant coal miners, many of whom had come from Ireland. They resisted recruitment efforts and attacked avowed loyalists, often disrupting mine operations in the process. In enacting its draft law, Pennsylvania conducted a census of its male population in order to meet its quota. Married men ages twenty to thirty-five and bachelors thirty-five to forty-five were designated "Category 1." Married men thirty-five to forty-five were assigned to "Category 2." Access to employee records, such as those provided by Smith, made the census easier to accomplish. Draft resistance in mine country grew. Men stopped work and protested conscription.

Smith's murder and attacks on draft officials, combined with rumors that miners were forming a pro-Confederacy resistance, brought matters to a head just as the 10ᵗʰ New Jersey reached the scene. The 10ᵗʰ wasted little time in acting, rounding up 106 "suspects" who were sent to Reading to stand trial.

"The Irish gangs resist all soldiers brought against them," Cape May Countian Charles Coward wrote. The miners were said to have denigrated the soldiers as "white slaves of Abraham Lincoln." "Hanging is too good for them," Coward concluded.

Soldiers converged on mines, covering exits. Miners emerging from the bowels of the earth were name-checked. If the name appeared on a "wanted" list, the man was arrested.

Trials in Reading were relocated to Mauch Chunk in February 1864. Fines and prison terms were handed out for "conspiracy to resist the draft," enraging miners. Talk circulated that they would take the soldiers' guns, raise a regiment and join Lee's army.

Company B at Mauch Chunk moved seventy-five prisoners from jail and "put them on a train for Fort Mifflin," wrote Donnelly. "The soldiers waited until the women were in bed," he added, "because they would carry on too much if they knew we were taking their men away." Even so, the company was greeted at the depot by a crowd of hundreds, blocking the train.

While at Mauch Chunk, Donnelly recalled, there were two court-martial trials, the sentences of which were carried out under orders of Captain Claypool. "We shaved their heads and branded them on the foreheads," after which the band struck up the "rogue's march" and turned them loose.

Beatings and killings. Strikes and draft resistance. Rumors of armed insurrection and treason. It all made for splashy headlines. One newspaperman, Benjamin Bannon, editor of the *Miner's Journal*, pushed one of the nicknames for his designated villains. Donnelly's journal recorded the nickname: "Molly Maguires."

Violent protests greeted efforts to conduct a census to determine eligible candidates. When the list of eligibles was published, men left the collieries in protest. One aspect of the draft, exemption for purchasing a substitute, especially rankled the miners, none of whom possessed financial wherewithal to "qualify" for a "Get Out of Draft" card. This, combined with general disdain for the Emancipation Proclamation, fueled anger and disorder throughout the anthracite region.

Lists were stolen. Threats were made. Shots rang out in the night. A provost marshal was murdered. A train carrying draftees to the front was stopped by five hundred armed men. Anyone wishing to leave the train was encouraged to do so.

In April 1864, the 10th rejoined the Army of the Potomac at Brandy Station, now part of the 1st Jersey Brigade, just in time for Grant's push toward Richmond. Among those were men from the county including Elias Scull, Tenbrook Price and John Wright.

Scull, a corporal, originally signed up in October 1861, but according to Stryker's *Record of New Jersey Civil War Soldiers*, he "deserted" in December of that year. However, he returned to duty two years later and served until July 1865.

Price's father was Reverend Jacob Price, a Methodist clergyman from Dennisville. Reverend Price was deeply involved with Methodist revival camps. When Jesse Diverty retired from running the camp meeting at South Seaville, Reverend Price took charge. His son, Tenbrook, fought as corporal in Company B. Upon completing his three-year enlistment, he reenlisted in February 1864, serving until January 1865.

A number of veterans reenlisted, likely influenced by a notice Donnelly recalled reading: "President Lincoln said all those who served two years and over, might re-enlist and would receive $402." Aaron Moore and Samuel Morton from Dennisville re-upped, as did Corporal Joseph Abrahams, who was subsequently wounded in action in October.

Another Dennisville man, Sergeant Mathias Creamer, rejoined and, in May 1865, died of chronic diarrhea at Sutherland Station, Virginia, where there'd been a major battle a month earlier.

Reenlistment papers of these and other men referred to their unit as the "10th New Jersey Veteran Volunteers." The 10th fought at the Battle of the Wilderness and Spotsylvania. Donnelly recalled the regiment's experience in the Wilderness. "We crossed the Rapidan and started out on a wood road and soon heard shooting going on in the timber."

The 10th was ordered to the right flank into that timber amid thick fire and smoke. The men encountered the Rebel line in what became "seven days of continuous fight." On May 6, the regiment lost almost an entire company, taken prisoner during an attack by Rebel general John Gordon. On May 8, another 80 men were captured. These men were actually rescued before being imprisoned. These losses came in addition to 113 killed or wounded.

Heavy losses continued at Cold Harbor, where the 10th held the third line, losing seventy men the first day. One of those killed was re-enlistee Joseph Layton from Tuckahoe.

Sunday, May 12, was "marching day," according to Donnelly. "If we could out march Lee's army about ten miles, we could march right into Richmond without any opposition." Instead, the Rebels shelled them. Claypool was wounded in the shoulder and left behind while the company advanced. As the Rebels counterattacked, they were ordered to lie down and then "double-quicked" into the thickest timber, firing as they moved. They ceased firing in response to shouts from ahead that "we were firing on our own men." A rebel ruse. But in the confusion of the dense woods, Company B avoided capture.

Next night, the 10th moved to an area Donnelly called the "slaughter pen," near Spotsylvania Court House. An artillery duel commenced, with charges and countercharges. "Grant's whole army charged at the same time." Reinforcements arrived the following day. The offensive resumed, but with no success. Trench warfare in the pouring rain continued for the next eleven days. "If a man's head happened to go up, he was shot by a sharpshooter."

"At night we would go out hunting for the dead men's knapsacks and would run across the rebels doing the same thing," Donnelly wrote. "We would run back to our trench and the rebels would retreat for theirs.…Dead artillery horses lying all around, tops of trees shot off and the trunks looked like splint brooms. We were so tired I had to put tobacco in my eyes to stay awake." Samuel Morton of Dennisville was killed in action and buried at Fredericksburg. That summer, the 10th again transferred, this time to the Shenandoah Valley, where it participated in the Battle of Winchester. The regiment joined a force holding Jubal Early's superior numbers in check for six hours. August 17, 1864, began with a bugle call, according to William Donnelly. The regiment moved down the valley to a peach orchard near a farmhouse. With Donnelly in charge of a platoon, they crossed a meadow to a rail fence, where they met Confederates, who fired and then retreated while a battery raked the company, driving back the federals. Donnelly found cover on the ground as Rebels overran their position.

Donnelly was taken prisoner. Another prisoner of war was Elvy Creamer of Dennisville. Another January re-upper, Creamer was sent to Andersonville, where he succumbed to diarrhea in August 1864, the same ailment that would take his brother Mathias in 1865. Mathias had rejoined the 10th with his brother on the same day, January 20, 1864. "I was half a mile inside enemy lines and saw our flag fall into the hands of the enemy." Donnelly recalled. They also took Donnelly's hat, coat, pants and money. "We turned our colors over to General [John B.] Gordon and were marched off." Donnelly shared his meager supply of coffee with his guards.

On August 20, the prisoners were moved toward Stanton and the next day were finally fed rations of flour, with the men frying the half-rolled dough. The prisoners plotted escape with the aid of their guards, who griped they were "tired of the war." Unfortunately, they were marched out of camp before they could make a break and were loaded on a train headed south. Eventually, Donnelly was sent to prison at Danville, "number six on the second floor of a tobacco warehouse."

By the end of the Winchester engagement, the regiment that had joined the Army of the Potomac at over six hundred strong had been reduced to eighty effectives. These veterans, along with recent recruits, were returned to Petersburg for the war's duration.

Rebel desertions skyrocketed. The morale of those coming across reflected flagging spirits of the once indomitable Army of Northern Virginia. Richmond and Petersburg were being evacuated, deserters claimed. The army was "disgusted" with Jeff Davis's government. These desertions dramatically improved Union morale.

In February, more than 1,000 Confederates quit. In the first three weeks of March, another 1,800 deserted. Lines occupied by the 10th Regiment experienced desertions of more than 500 men from the Confederate 3rd Corps. Reenlisting remnants of the 10th hoped to see the war through to victory. One of those reenlisting was Silas Hoffman, Company I. He stayed with the regiment until July 1, 1865. He was there when Union forces finally broke through at Petersburg on April 2. Horace Bickley of Company K was there too. He'd originally signed for three years in October 1861 and re-upped on February 1, 1865.

Back home, Sergeant Bickley had taught at Union School in Dennis Township. After the war, he became a postmaster.

Donnelly was taken prisoner three times during the war. He survived, mustering out on July 1, 1865. After the war, he moved to Pasadena, California. Last survivor of the 10th Regiment, Donnelly died on July 16, 1934. On his deathbed, according to his obituary, he asked his daughter to bring an American flag to his bedside. "The only legacy I leave my children is that grand old flag," he reportedly said.

FAMILY TIES

While many in the county traced ancestors back to the *Mayflower*, Richard Swain Thompson did them one better, following his family tree roots to the area's original inhabitants, the Lenni Lenape, and even to royalty—Nummy, the last "king" to live in Cape May County. Actually, Nummy's sister.

She had a Lenape name but was better known as Snow Flower. She married an English missionary named Benijah Thompson, who baptized her and, for reasons best known to Thompson, renamed her Prudence. Whenever Benijah wasn't fighting in the American Revolution as New Jersey militia captain, he and Prudence brought children into the world. The third of eight was Richard, who later fought the British as a militia captain in the War of 1812. He would become grandfather to Richard S. Thompson.

Grandfather Thompson did his share to intermingle the family name with those of other county yeoman families, marrying three times—a Swain, a Price and a Leaming. The first marriage produced four children, including a second-generation Richard Thompson, born in 1795. His third marriage resulted in one child, Sarah, who would one day marry Nathaniel Holmes.

In addition to the family farm at Green Creek, the second Richard held shipping interests and was politically active. His second marriage, to Elizabeth Holmes, member of the Holmes-Hand branch of that locally important family, produced five children—four daughters and one son, Richard Swain Thompson. In all, Thompson's marriages linked families with a Leaming

(Richard Swain Thompson's sister Hannah married Dr. Coleman Leaming) and a Falkinburg (sister Isabelle married Joseph Falkinburg Leaming), as well as Swain, Hand, Holmes and other families.

R.S.T. would further complicate the web, marrying Catherine Scovil after the war. Her uncle (by marriage) was brother to Joseph Falkinburg Leaming, who being married to Thompson's sister made her uncle her brother-in-law. Imagining the strains of "I Am My Own Grandpa" about now? Welcome to nineteenth-century genealogy Cape May County–style. All of this is intended to demonstrate how interconnected county families were. Relationships underscore much of the enlistment activity among county men during the war years.

Richard Swain Thompson was born into modest affluence on December 27, 1837, in Cape May Court House. As the youngest child and only son, he lived at Woodside, homestead of his grandfather Nathaniel Holmes. In 1823, Holmes sold Woodside to his soon to be son-in-law, Thompson's father. The Thompson family would live there until 1878, when Richard Swain Thompson sold the property to *his* brother-in-law, Dr. Coleman Leaming (married to Hannah).

Woodside's history goes back to the earliest days of Cape May County settlement as part of an estate owned by Shamgar Hand, an original white settler of the area. Thompson was descended from Hand on his mother's side. There was a significant gap in age between the boy and his four elder sisters. Elizabeth, the youngest of the four, was thirteen when Richard came along.

Thompson's father was a man of considerable local importance. At various times, he served as a member of the County Board of Freeholders representing Middle Township. He also held the offices of county clerk and sheriff. By the time of Richard's birth, he'd moved up to elected posts at the state level.

His father, determining that his son required a "gentleman's education," dispatched Richard, age thirteen, to Treemont, a religious boarding school in Norristown. Richard attended for four years. His father next arranged with Reverend Alden Scovil for the boy to attend boarding school near Trenton. It was here that Swain Thompson

Richard Swain Thompson, lieutenant colonel, 12th New Jersey Volunteer Infantry, grew up in Cape May Court House. *Dennis Township Old School House Museum.*

first met his future wife. The object of this schooling was to prepare the boy for a career in law.

In 1857, the senior Thompson died at Woodside. Richard, now twenty, was on his own as far as finishing his education. He received a career "assist" when Jeremiah Leaming, another (distant) relation, arranged for Richard to read law in the Philadelphia law office of Asa Fish. He did so until 1859, when he left Philadelphia for Harvard College of Law.

While at Harvard, Richard was exposed to fomenting social issues of the day. Hot-button topics included merits of the recently formed Republican Party, states' rights, secession, slavery and, of course, the looming likelihood of civil war. Youthful talk and writing touched on such lofty subjects as the future of civilization, free government and humanity itself. "Either there must be a withdraw on the part of seceding states or there will be a collision between their forces and those of the government," William Potter wrote to Thompson on March 9, 1861, about a month before shots were fired at Fort Sumter. Potter was a Bridgeton native and Harvard classmate. It was during this time that Thompson's skills as a public speaker emerged. Use of language, ranging his voice, his personal bearing—all would come into play in the near future.

Enthusiasm for war in the aftermath of Fort Sumter turned pro-Southern countians into rabid Unionists, eager to smash secession. Although he failed to win the state in 1860, Lincoln carried Cape May County, as did Republican candidates for every spot up for election. The First Congressional District elected pro-Lincoln Republican John Nixon. The *Cape May Ocean Wave*, promoting a decidedly pro-Union slant, denounced the "fiendish Jeff Davis and Company firing the first shots."

An April 27, 1861 meeting at Cape May Court House ended with a resolution: "We will stand by our state and national government to maintain the union, the constitution and the laws, and protect our national flag from further insult."

Richard Thompson enlisted on April 23, 1861, in Company I of an artillery unit in Philadelphia. The move was likely inspired by his brother-in law John Stevenson, a captain in the 3rd Pennsylvania Artillery, and followed up on Lincoln's first call for seventy-five thousand volunteers, to fight what most Northerners believed would be a short war.

While Thompson drilled with his unit, renamed Company A, 1st Regiment Light Artillery Philadelphia Home Guards, he continued preparing for the bar. Meanwhile, the ill-prepared Union army suffered a shocking thrashing at Manassas (Bull Run). It became apparent that the war would not end as quickly as first believed.

Thompson passed his bar examination in March 1862 just as his year's enlistment drew to a close, but his experiences with the Union army were just beginning.

On July 7, 1862, the call went out throughout the North for 300,000 volunteers to serve three years. Instead of creating new divisions for urgently needed new troops, regiments were assigned to existing divisions. The 12th New Jersey Regiment joined the 2nd Brigade, 3rd Division.

The first man to actively recruit for the 12th was Edward Stratton, a prosperous merchant from Gloucester County. Stratton advertised in the *Woodbury Constitution*, "JERSEYMEN TO THE RESCUE." The notice promised twenty-five-dollar advance bonuses while appealing to readers' then red-hot patriotic fervor. While the Woodbury recruiting office was *not* swamped with volunteers, there was a large enlistment turnout of Strattons. Edward's younger brother James, along with four cousins—William, Emanuel, Charles and Azariah—enlisted. The first three of these would die in combat. The fourth, Azariah, would survive the war and become a farmer at Beeseley's Point.

That same month, Thompson and friend Potter secured positions with the Union volunteer army through New Jersey governor Charles Olden. Back home, the *Ocean Wave* trumpeted the announcement. "Richard S Thompson Esq of Cape May Court House, true Jersey man and son of Cape May, has been commissioned a captain by Gov, Olden, to raise a company for the 12th regiment."

One of Thompson's first assignments was addressing a mass rally at Bridgeton, encouraging enlistment. According to his hometown paper, he recruited twenty men before returning to Cape May County looking for more. The paper praised Thompson's enthusiasm displayed at Bridgeton, where a company was filled "in about ten days" and already prepared to join the regiment at its Woodbury camp. The paper called on the governor to ask for more regiments to accommodate other men wanting to enlist.

"The people of Cape May are just arousing to the call," the writer noted, suggesting that two more regiments could easily be filled. He also warned that, in the event of a draft, "cowards and traitors" hoping to shirk their duty by obtaining "Certificates of their inability" wouldn't be so easily able to avoid serving, as physical ability to do so "would be decided by a surgeon appointed for that purpose."

Rallies were held in other parts of south Jersey, especially Bridgeton. There, Congressman John Nixon was joined by Thompson and Port Norris physician Howard Willetts. Willetts was grandson of Nicholas

Dr. Howard Willets (*far left*) outside his office in Cumberland County in 1887. *Dennis Township Old School House Museum.*

Willetts, former state legislator from Dias Creek. His father was Dr. Reuben Willetts. Howard attended West Point. While he did not graduate, he excelled in certain areas, including tactics. Willetts *did* graduate from Jefferson Medical College in 1858 and, like his father, Reuben, became a doctor.

Willetts was something of a rarity among the fledgling officers. Not only was he a doctor, but he had also already experienced combat command with the 7th Regiment, in Virginia during McClellan's ill-fated Peninsula Campaign. Captain Willetts, at the Battle of Williamsburg, led his company of the 7th in such a manner as to save the unit from being wiped out. He was wounded in the chest and hand. In another action, his head was nearly separated from his shoulders by a heavy artillery shell. Despite his multiple wounds and near scrapes with death, Willetts wished to return to action, preferably at a higher rank. His wish was granted when Governor Olden named him lieutenant colonel of the 12th.

Back in Court House, Thompson recruited in his home county, authorized to raise Company K, for which he'd be elected captain. The speech making, drum rolling, flag waving and bonfire rallying was effective. The ranks of Company K quickly filled. By midsummer, Captain Thompson and company had reported to Woodbury and the newly established Camp Stockton, joining 12th New Jersey Volunteer Infantry.

In early September, the 12th Regiment officially mustered into the U.S. Army with 850 officers and enlisted men, most of them from south Jersey. The *Ocean Wave* September 4 described the 12th's "fine time last night at Camp Stockton in Woodbury." A "sumptuous dinner" was provided by citizens of Gloucester and Salem Counties, and a presentation following of regimental and U.S. flags by Congressman John Nixon, accepted for the regiment by Captain Thompson, who addressed a crowd of three thousand.

Most recruits came to Camp Stockton as farmers, but the south Jersey enlistees brought along many other skills as tradesmen: blacksmiths, farriers, shoemakers, fishermen, millers, harness makers, coopers, oyster men, clerks and barkeeps—even an undertaker. All were anxious and eager and had not a clue of what awaited them.

Families, friends, fiancées and general well-wishers gathered to see them off when they headed to war in late September. Amid flowing tears and martial music, fireworks and fiery speeches, they boarded a train, many for the first time, heading south and stopping at Baltimore before reaching camp at Ellicott's Mills, Maryland, where they were stationed for four months.

In his diary, Thompson described the circuitous route taken, including a stop at Camden, where he briefly rendezvoused with his future wife. Across the river at Philadelphia, they ate at Cooper's Refreshment Saloon. "We then marched to Broad Street Depot to take cars to Baltimore. Arrive at Baltimore at 11:30 p.m....march from one depot to another with guns loaded and bayonets fixed [Baltimore was considered pro-Southern]."

They slept on the street until the following afternoon before taking the train to their final destination. Waiting for them nearby, according to "reports," was Stonewall Jackson. The men were ordered "to arms" after midnight. Some companies drew guard duty, while others marched out "quick time" five miles but found no enemy.

This process was repeated several times before martial law was declared. On September 12, Thompson was appointed assistant provost marshal. Local citizens were not happy. "Woe be to the secesh falling into his hands," the *Ocean Wave* predicted.

"Administering oaths and granting passes," Thompson wrote, describing his duties. "Many refuse to take the oath. Arrest several citizens." That was just the first week.

Much of their time in Maryland passed in drilling—constant, repetitive drilling. The men learned how to move in a body, coordinating movement, acting as one. It worked well on the drill field, especially after the Jersey farm boys learned to distinguish right from left.

The county paper led cheers for their men in the field. "The rebels counted on the sympathies of New Jersey and intimated she would secede with them. How fully their expectations have been realized may be seen by the fact that she has just organized her 25th regiment of infantry…all without a draft.…Our quota of 300,000 three-year men is now in the field, made up without any postponement of the draft.…New Jersey is all right!"

New Jersey was *not*, the paper went on, refuting other descriptions of the state—"a monopoly-ridden state in the breeches pocket of her politicians; the 'State of Camden and Amboy' [the state's railroad monopoly]; her people half a century behind any other…a good state to emigrate *from*."

That first winter away from home, the Jersey boys figured out one way to ward off chills. They built a cider press, which produced "Jersey Lightning," apple jack peculiar to the Garden State.

The 12th had its first look at the enemy when companies under Lieutenant Colonel Willetts took charge of a trainload of prisoners at Frederick, Maryland. Thompson wrote to his sister Hannah on the condition of the men under his charge: "1400 gray backs…they were poorly dressed, some without shoes or hats and they were covered with lice, body and head." The 12th also encountered runaway slaves for the first time. "Our men make them sing 'nigger' songs," Thompson wrote.

Otherwise, camp life meant constant drilling, picket details and occasional provost work that called on Thompson's legal acumen, such as sentencing deserters who were dispatched to Baltimore (and jail). On October 20, Thompson enjoyed his first opportunity to command the entire regiment during drill, while his nights passed, dining on oyster suppers with local loyalists and socializing with the ladies.

In November 1862, the regiment learned that Lincoln had replaced McClellan with Ambrose Burnside. And New Jersey elected a new governor: Democrat Joel Parker. Parker was not perceived as "friendly" to the troops in the field, most of whom likely would have voted for Marcus Ward, known as the "Soldier's Friend" for his efforts to support the state's volunteer warriors. *Likely* is the key word—soldiers in the field were not permitted to vote.

The *other* big news was the Proclamation. Lincoln had freed the slaves in rebelling states, effective January 1, 1863. Feelings were mixed. Many soldiers had volunteered to preserve the Union and punish traitors. There was little desire to die to free slaves. Most men of the 12th had experienced little or no contact with Black people, slave or free. Still, some saw eradication of slavery as a worthy objective for carrying the war to a successful conclusion.

Slavery, in their minds, was an "immoral abomination." Their religious upbringing, though perhaps not particularly outspoken on the issue, at least suggested that true Christianity could not coexist with the peculiar institution. The men weren't happy with the inaugural address of their state's new governor. Parker lambasted Lincoln for the army's failure to date, saying that the president was more interested in freeing slaves than defeating Rebels. "Peace should be sought," Parker asserted, and states' rights "recognized." The Union should be restored to what it was before the war. His Democratic Party, which then controlled the state legislature, passed resolutions formalizing sentiments expressed in his address.

Adding insult to injury for troops doing the fighting, the legislature voted down a measure pushed by their peers from the Southern section of the state that would permit combat soldiers to vote.

The men in the regiment agreed on one point. The 12th would fight until a final victory was won. The regiment was finally issued American-made muskets, a vast improvement over the antiques they'd been using in drill. Since the Union army started with a small supply of weapons, the government bought any guns available. This was before Northern industry kicked into full war production mode. Those first weapons were older, heavy and cumbersome to handle. They proved to be inefficient in the type of war that transpired. The adoption of the rifled musket improved the range and firepower of the infantry.

The new musket still lacked long-range accuracy but was deadly at short range (a point that would become of great importance at Gettysburg). In place of the Minié ball, it fired rounds consisting of metal balls and three charges of buckshot—four times as many chances to hit a target.

Other changes occurred toward the end of the year. Finally, on December 6, the 12th received orders to move out. No train rides this time. The men would be marching, joining the Army of the Potomac above Richmond. "Settling bills and writing letters to my friends…snow on the ground and weather very cold," Thompson prepared to leave camp.

They marched sixty *muddy* miles. While the regiment plodded through morass to join Ambrose Burnside, his army was busily engaged in its disastrous effort at Fredericksburg. The 12th arrived afterward, following a twenty-mile march to camp at Falmouth.

While at Falmouth, Thompson encountered a number of familiar faces from the county, assigned to other regiments, including George Smith from the 7th and Dr. John Wiley, Thompson family physician and Court House neighbor, assigned to the 6th. Thompson also met up with a distant relative, Franklin Hand, 6th Regiment. Hand would soon be discharged for health reasons.

Writing home, Thompson reported that he felt homesick but "could not remain inactive while my country is in danger," a sentiment shared by most men in the volunteer army.

Soldier morale was low after Fredericksburg. Living conditions at camp didn't improve lagging spirits. The ill-fitting, uncomfortable uniforms were apparently designed with a one-size-fits-all mindset. Shoes posed the same problem, at least when the soldiers *had* shoes. Sickness plagued the camp, including smallpox. Many soldiers succumbed to illness during winter months. In addition, soldiers weren't being paid, so money wasn't being sent to needy families back home. Many men took "French leave," going AWOL to head north to visit their families. These conditions worsened after the Mud March, Burnside's last futile effort to regain the offensive. Those who remained endured freezing wind and snow, alternating with skin-soaking rain.

"I have never in my life saw such roads," one soldier wrote home. "Seventy thousand men trudging through mud up to their knees. Bawling teamsters, broken wagons. Dying horses."

While the war-weary army suffered in camp, licking its wounds, a big shakeup occurred at the top with "Fighting" Joe Hooker replacing Burnside. Hooker took a number of immediate steps to restore the strength and morale of an army reeling from a series of defeats: improved clothing and rations, a revamped leave schedule and a team spirit gimmick, assigning distinctive badges to various corps to wear on their uniforms.

The 12th wore blue trefoils, the trefoil resembling the club suit in a deck of playing cards. The regiment also created its own rallying cry: "Clubs are trump."

Hooker planned the next operation to unfold at a place called Chancellorsville. By early spring of 1863, Hooker's efforts to rejuvenate the Army of the Potomac were showing positive effect. And there were command changes in the 12th. In March, Willetts was promoted to colonel, and later that month, it was announced that a new officer would soon join the regiment.

Sergeant Richard Townsend, from Dennisville, had been promoted to second lieutenant, Company C. Then assigned to the 10th Regiment, Townsend would not actually assume his new commission until the end of June. Meanwhile, the Army of the Potomac was on the move.

On April 28, seventy thousand infantrymen crossed the Rappahannock River above Fredericksburg, moving into the densely overgrown area known as the Wilderness. Hooker intended to push through this inhospitable place toward open ground before Lee responded. At first, all went as planned until Hooker actually encountered opposition. He then halted the advance, that hesitation giving his opponent the opening he'd been waiting for. The Rebels pounced.

On May 3, the 12th experienced its baptism of fire, what soldiers called "seeing the elephant." Facing the seasoned troops of Stonewall Jackson, the regiment lost 24 men killed, 132 wounded and 22 missing and presumed captured. Fighting had broken out all around the regiment. Even before the 12th engaged, other units were breaking for the rear. The Federal position quickly dissolved in confusion as infantry raced through the lines while the 12th held. Colonel Willetts ordered the men to form a line of battle in thicket and briars, where it remained until evening.

Not one shot was fired. Richard Thompson recalled the battle as it resumed the following day: "May 2. Monday morning. Our artillery opens heavy fighting all day.…Afternoon fight opens on the right. Our brigade passed down Plank Road. Several of our regiment are wounded.…Our brigade was in line of balls and shells all night. Artillery and infantry firing over us."

Terse writing, but the action was lively. The Rebels hit them with everything, cannon balls and musketry, for four hours. Enemies seemed to lurk behind every tree, firing at them from every direction—the combat-seasoned army of Stonewall Jackson. This type of fighting was a harrowing new experience for the regiment, trained to fight in the open.

Union troops gave way. The 12th was ordered to support another regiment about to break. Plugging a gap in the line hardest hit by the assault, Willetts organized his men. Once in place, he ordered them to lie on their bellies and wait. Enemy shots buzzed over and around them. Finally, Willetts led them back to their original position near the Chancellor House.

On Sunday, May 3, the 12th was again sent to support troops confronting Jackson's army, now under the command of Jeb Stuart, Jackson having been mortally wounded the night before. The regiment had just settled into position when the enemy attacked. The Rebels treated the 12th to an eerie, wailing sound, a spine-tingling cry the Jersey boys heard for the first time in their lives: the Rebel yell.

When the attackers reached two hundred yards distant, the 12th opened fire. They hurriedly reloaded as the enemy closed. The cumbersome procedure seemed to take forever. Some failed to properly reload. Some were so stunned by the reality of combat that they froze. Others simply pulled the trigger without making the effort to reload. They enjoyed some success, singling out targets once the enemy drew within closer range on more open ground. But still, the Rebels came.

The regiment took casualties but held its ground, clearing the front of attackers. Then a second assault, larger than the first, firing as it surged toward them. Standing in front of the breastworks, waving his sword to urge his men to fight, Willetts went down, a rifle ball in his right arm. The line wavered as the attack now came from two directions. Also wounded was one of the Strattons, Edward, a captain, hit by two bullets as he tried to rally the regiment to hold while other units broke for the rear. One bullet glanced off his skull, and the other hit his knee.

Another Stratton witnessed the scene. Edward's cousin Azariah, mustered as a corporal in Company F in 1862, was the third of four brothers to join that company. He was promoted to sergeant in December 1862, first sergeant in January 1864 and finally first lieutenant in September of that year.

Unlike brother Corporal Henry (killed during the raid on Bliss Farm at Gettysburg), Charles (killed at Spotsylvania, shot through the head at age seventeen) or Emanuel (severely wounded at Chancellorsville and discharged after a year in hospital), Azariah survived the war and all the battles in which the 12th was engaged. In 1865, he was promoted to captain, a commission formerly held by his cousin. Azariah held that rank

Sergeant Azariah Stratton, 12th New Jersey Volunteer Infantry, settled on a farm at Beeseley's Point in Upper Township after the war. *Upper Township Historical Society.*

at Appomattox, where he witnessed Lee's surrender. After the war, he returned to New Jersey and married before settling on a farm in Beeseley's Point (Upper Township). There, he raised "vegetables, chickens, and boys," according to William P. Haines in his *History of the Men of Company F.*

Haines wrote about Azariah's demeanor during their time together in combat. "He shared our joys and sorrows and never got lost but once [Falmouth at the beginning of the war]. He caught one of his men asleep on picket duty in the face of the enemy and didn't report him…for if he had, the penalty [for the sleeper] was death…and *these lines would have never been written.*"

Haines described Azariah as "sturdy, possessing a bravery without rashness and participated in every battle and skirmish. Though his clothing was pierced by many bullets, he never missed a drill, roll call, or mess and came home with the love and respect of every man who ever served with or under him."

All around, men fell, wounded or killed. Their resolve to stand and fight weakened. The unit to its right broke, racing for the rear. Ignoring desperate shouted orders of officers to hold, the 12th melted away as well. "Our brigade was outflanked," Thompson wrote. "The right of the 12th gave way. The remainder of the 12th and a detachment of the 108th New York held their ground and repulsed the enemy."

At this point, Thompson commanded the remaining troops, leading the successful fight to stop the enemy advance. He added that he'd been "slightly wounded on the wrist." "The rebels must have been fed on gunpowder and whisky and are more like fiends than men," he recalled in a letter home to his sister.

After the retreat, there was an unsettled quiet, The Jersey men had killed and been killed. Combat produced a psychic shock resulting in protracted silence in the ranks. Finally, the 12th withdrew in the rain, returning to the river crossing. Marching in the rain, the regiment reached camp at Falmouth, exhausted and demoralized and changed forever.

To the again defeated Army of the Potomac, Lee's Army of Northern Virginia seemed invincible. Perhaps the Rebels felt that way too, including their commanding general. While the Federals licked their wounds, Lee made plans to take the offensive and bring the war north into Pennsylvania.

The *Ocean Wave* reported that Thompson, visiting home on leave, talked about his experience in the recent battle at Chancellorsville, noting that the 12th did "valiant service though it was their first experience on the battlefield."

According to the reporter, Thompson did not consider it a defeat. "He considers the damage to the enemy five to our one. The principal cause of Hooker's retreat was the retreat of Sedgwick at the city of Fredericksburg, which endangered Hooker's communications."

"'The army is by no means demoralized,' Thompson continued, 'and were exceedingly loth to leave when the order was given to fall back.'" Rather than pursue the Federals, according to Thompson, the Rebels were "nowhere to be seen." "The battle was the 'greatest wound the rebel army has yet suffered' and the army had 'utmost confidence in General Hooker.'"

That same edition of the paper reported on the status of another officer of the 12th, Colonel Willets: "severely wounded in the left wrist in the last battle is in Philadelphia and it is feared he will lose his hand….[N]ot the colonel's first wound, he having received several in former engagements in another regiment [7th]. We have been informed that this is his twelfth wound." The paper added that when Willetts was compelled to leave the field, R.S. Thompson, "acting major," assumed command of the regiment.

Eventually, the men would agree that their defeat at Chancellorsville was not due to their own lack of will or valor but rather failure at the top of command. They wanted another go at the Rebels. They'd soon get their chance. Lee moved north during the sultry weeks of June, through Maryland and the Shenandoah Valley and into Pennsylvania, never sure when or where he might encounter the enemy. His plan was audacious enough. Invade the North and attack Philadelphia, perhaps even Washington. Compel the Union to sue for peace and recognize the sovereignty of the Confederacy.

Meanwhile, the defeated Hooker gave way to George Meade as commander of the Army of the Potomac. Meade's plan was to pursue Lee, cut his supply and communication lines and bring him to open battle. Neither general knew quite where the other was or where they might meet. Shoes, or the Rebels' lack of them, perhaps decided the latter question. Upon learning that a quantity of supplies, especially shoes, had been stored for the Union army near Gettysburg, Lee's army barefooted that way. The Union army followed.

On the march north, the heat was so oppressive and water so scarce that men dropped out of line and collapsed. Crossing Bull Run battlefield, they saw decaying bodies of dead soldiers. One corpse, its arm protruding from a hastily dug grave, hand outstretched, provoked rare laughter. "See boys, the soldier's putting out his hand for back pay."

Azariah Stratton recalled that, nearing Gettysburg, "couriers bring news that our forces are being whipped." They then heard sounds like thunder, artillery fire, and started toward it "at a quick." By the time the 12th reached Pennsylvania late July 1, night was falling, but the Battle of Gettysburg was on. "We went into line on a gentle incline and could witness the formation in the valley between the two armies," Thompson wrote. "At 4:45 pm, the artillery from both sides opened fire and continued on our left until dark."

Bliss Farm was located in a swale about five hundred yards from Rebel lines. The enemy used farm buildings as a forward post while they massed along Seminary Ridge. Built on a rock foundation, topped by sturdy oak, Bliss barn proved an ideal fortress for Mississippi sharpshooters. They opened up on Union skirmishers, pinning them down on Cemetery Ridge.

Union sharpshooters, using long-range rifles with scopes placed on tripods, were dispatched to engage them. This slowed the enemy attack, as the Rebels dove for cover whenever they spotted the flash of a gun before reappearing to fire back.

According to Thompson's *A Scrap at Gettysburg*, Union marksmen formed squads of three. "One man would fire. The enemy would duck. Then his partners would fire at the opening where they anticipated the enemy reappearing…just in time to catch the bullets."

The 12th was initially positioned as skirmishers behind stone walls along Emmitsburg Road. After several failed attempts to take the strongly held Rebel position, companies of the 12th relieved attacking units from Pennsylvania.

Under a blistering summer sun and unrelenting fire from assorted places, especially that barn, several officers fell wounded or killed. Still, the 12th moved forward toward the barn, holding fire until within close range. Finally, the Jerseyans fired a volley, causing defenders to flee or surrender. Bluecoats rushed from cellar to loft, clearing the building of enemy shooters. In the process of taking the barn, the regiment lost forty killed or wounded.

According to Samuel Toombs in *New Jersey Troops at Gettysburg*, "No bolder attack was made upon that well-contested field and it decisively gave the regiment a reputation for gallantry which it never lost." But they did lose control of the barn. Rebel artillery took dead aim at the farm buildings, destroying several, but not the barn. The Mississippians returned, forcing the outnumbered Jerseyans to withdraw. Confederate sharpshooters resumed their harassing fire.

The morning of July 3, Captain Thompson, doing temporary duty as major, was ordered to retake the barn. Choosing his own Company K as part of the five-company assault force, he led the advance at a steady walk toward the barn. Then they charged, over stone walls and through fields, until reaching their target. Vigorous fighting ensued during which twenty were wounded, but the bluecoats retook the barn. Another Stratton boy, Will, was mortally wounded.

The enemy counterattacked again in great numbers. Again the Federals couldn't hold the barn. Upon retreating to their own line, men were asked why they didn't burn the annoying barn. "No one recalled being ordered to do so," Azariah Stratton recalled.

Among the 12th's casualties during the taking of Bliss's barn was Second Lieutenant Richard Henry Townsend, from Dennisville. This was Townsend's first command with the 12th. Townsend was born on June 13, 1839, in North Dennis, third child and eldest son of William and Hannah Smith Ludlam Townsend, both descended from prominent families. William

Smith Townsend was a wealthy landowner, businessman and political figure, a freeholder member from Dennis Township. His interests included a glass making factory in Port Elizabeth. He owned extensive land in the center of the county and was an active proponent of bringing the railroad into the county (and presumably across his holdings).

The Townsends were Quakers and, as with many in that religious sect, faced a dilemma with the war: fight to preserve the Union or heed the injunction of their faith and "keep out of quarrels and strife that arise in the world and concern not yourselves with them." Young men wishing to enlist faced harsh criticism from parents and co-religionists even to the point of expulsion from meeting and shunning by families. Some were disinherited altogether. Available information suggests that William Townsend was not opposed to the Union cause. As a county freeholder, Townsend advocated bonus payments to enlistees and support for families left in need when wage earners went off to fight.

The Townsend home in North Dennisville, known as Five Chimneys, was the scene of many political gatherings. Townsend, once a member of the Whig Party, hosted national Whig leader Henry Clay when the oft-unsuccessful presidential candidate visited the county in 1848.

Townsend's wife, Hannah Smith Ludlam, daughter of Henry Ludlam Jr., traced lineage to Joseph Ludlam, original settler of the area. Through marriages of siblings to cousins over the years, the extended family was related to Falkinburgs, Leamings, Lawrences, Swains, Smiths and Holmes, much like the Thompsons of Cape May Court House.

At age twenty, Richard left the county to work as a seaman in Philadelphia. But he returned in June 1861 to marry Mary Tomlin of Goshen. Six months later, their son, Edwin, was born. Richard was not present for the birth, having enlisted on September 30 in the 10th Regiment, Company B, as a first sergeant.

Mary was daughter of John Tomlin, perhaps best known for his role in creating the Shunpike, an alternate route for local farmers taking produce to Cape Island, avoiding the toll road from Cape May Court House to the resort. Why had a recently married man and soon-to-be father enlisted in the army? Perhaps the prospect of steady pay to help support that new family. Perhaps in reaction to the patriotic fervor that swept the county at that time. Or maybe Richard simply wanted to get away and perform heroic deeds in combat.

Townsend joined his new regiment a few days before Gettysburg. He would be the only man from Company C and one of two officers of the 12th killed at Gettysburg. Thompson, who knew the family before the war, communicated with Richard's father, who was emotionally shattered by the news. Thompson also reported the news in a letter to his sister: "He was shot dead through the heart." Townsend was twenty-four years old.

He was buried in the first row, first grave, at Gettysburg National Cemetery. His family chose not to retrieve his remains. His father declined to attend Lincoln's speech commemorating the battlefield. His elder sister Annabelle went in his place. Richard's widow, Mary, moved in with her father until she eventually remarried.

Richard Townsend from North Dennis was killed at Gettysburg in his first engagement as an officer. *Dennis Township Old School House Museum.*

July 3 dawned, an oppressive stillness weighing over the battlefield. Artillery was silent. Skirmishers were inactive. Nature's hush before the storm's bursting fury. Awaiting inevitable onslaught, men tended to chores, making certain that the tools of their present occupation were in working order. Muskets were carefully checked and ammunition supplies replenished. "Like an ominous gathering of clouds, the enemy were moving great masses of troops," Thompson recalled. "We waited."

The 12th performed certain modifications to its ammo, rendering it more suitable for the encounter about to take place. Tearing open paper cartridges, men poured buckshot on the ground, replacing it with shot pellets. For close-up fighting, the shotgun effect would be far more deadly.

When the day's fighting started, Confederate artillery, 140 guns, opened a concentrated fire, blasting Union positions to soften them up while Rebel infantry massed. Thompson estimated that those guns fired twice per minute—280 shells per minute, 42,000 in two and a half hours. Loud? It was said that cannon fire could be heard in Philadelphia. "We made ourselves as little as possible on the ground," Azariah Stratton recalled. "But we couldn't lay in one position so we turned over on our backs and could trace the shells fly across overhead crossing every point on the compass."

"Shrieking shells burst everywhere," he continued. "Solid shot tore through the house and barn on our right. Cut off tree limbs in our rear." The line of the 12th was advanced to the front, some fifteen yards down slope from the crown of the ridge. "A majority of their shells passed overhead."

Tensely waiting, a soldier finally cried out, "Thank God. There comes the [Rebel] infantry." Anything that promised action was better than inaction under the horrors of that cannonade. Fifteen thousand Southerners, lines of march accompanied by blood-curdling Rebel yells, came right toward the 12th Regiment, positioned on the left of that oncoming human wave. The Rebels emerged from wooded cover on the slope of Seminary Ridge, advancing in double line of battle. On they came, banners flying, band playing, arms at right shoulder shift—all in plain sight of friend and foe. "Battle's magnificent stern array," Thompson wrote.

Azariah Stratton thought the Confederate advance "the grandest sight I ever saw…lines marching towards us, bayonets glistening in the sun, from right to left, far as the eye could see.…Their officers mounted, riding up and down the lines apparently keeping them in proper formation."

Even as so many were cut down, they maintained that orderly, forward movement, some walking, some trotting. All yelling. Nearer and nearer, they steadily marched, the Jersey men holding their fire. They'd learned something since becoming soldiers. Their muskets had no effectiveness when fired at distant targets.

As the Confederates drew within range, artillery opened up. Hundreds fell. But their lines converged, remaining solid without gaps. Union infantry, including the 12th, waited. The 12th was the only regiment armed with Springfield smoothbore muskets (.69-caliber), a fierce weapon at close range. As they awaited the enemy, the Federals felt confident in their reconfigured ammunition—a ball and three small buckshot, replacing them with buckshot pellets.

Finally, the Rebels were close enough, within forty yards. "Aim low," the order came. The regiment rose as a man from behind the wall and fired at point-blank range at many of the same men who'd bested them at Chancellorsville. A sheet of flame from four hundred men on the line sent the entire front attacking line down, while the mass in the rear pressed forward, only to meet a similar fate.

"Forward was annihilation," wrote Toombs. "To retreat is death."

Again and again, the Federals volleyed, reloading coolly and quickly. At points where Rebels reached the line, they fought hand to hand. Soon, the field was covered with dead and wounded Southerners, the rest retreating, the firepower of the 12th still pouring into them.

The Jersey men weren't finished. The threat in front repulsed, they turned to the flank and resumed firing. Rebels managed to reach within thirty feet of their line before they were repulsed. "They charged us with a division and a half of infantry with bayonets fixed," Richard Thompson wrote to his sisters. "We let their three lines come up within short range and our boys opened up on them." He added that the regiment took five hundred prisoners and "captured two stands of colors." "I cannot write a description of their charge or our fighting," he concluded. "Not over one-sixth the rebels who made the charge led by Longstreet and Hill went back. The ground is covered with their dead."

Not one attacker crossed the line of the 12th. The regiment's losses were considerable at twenty-three killed and eighty-three wounded.

At day's end, it started to rain. The next morning, the Army of Northern Virginia was gone. "I am well and uninjured, dirty and hungry," Thompson wrote July 5. The Army of the Potomac, having tasted victory, wanted more and was eager to move in pursuit.

Gettysburg changed the whole complexion of the war. Lee wasn't infallible. The Army of Northern Virginia wasn't invincible. The Yankees could stand and fight and *win*.

Big changes occurred on the homefront as well. The railroad finally arrived in Cape May County. It had taken years. The *Ocean Wave* proclaimed "A NEW ERA," announcing that the "last rail was laid on the Cape May and Millville Railroad." It predicted a bright future for the resort and the entire county, the "garden spot of the state."

One month earlier, the train was still beyond county limits, coming south to Port Elizabeth. But that summer, Cape May was connected by rail to the outside world. "On Monday last, our ears with a sound more welcome than the dinner bell at a first-class hotel…the whistle of the locomotive," according to the *Cape May Ocean Wave*.

Dr. Coleman Leaming, Thompson's brother-in-law, had lobbied to bring the train to Cape May. He also invested heavily in railroad bonds, investing Thompson's money as well. Thompson wrote to him in late July after hearing the news, expressing approval for Leaming's effort securing a depot site for Cape May Court House. But Thompson wouldn't be coming home anytime soon to enjoy a train ride.

Lee was once again well entrenched behind strong defensive works, south of the Rapidan River. Meanwhile, Meade appeared content to pass the summer in various camps. In early October, Lee decided to attack. After several days of skirmishing and maneuvering, the armies met at Bristoe Station. Once again, the 12th was one of the infantry units called on to counter.

The Jersey men charged, bayonets fixed, holding their musket fire until within close range. In doing so, they helped capture several Rebel cannons in a brief but fierce encounter. Thompson's recollection is, in places, jauntily descriptive, worthy of a seasoned combat vet with a taste for the romantic

Artist's rendering of West Jersey Railroad depot at Cape Island. *www.capemay.com/blog*

in war. "With a great hearty cheer that made the blood tremble, we received their infernal lead and sent back the battle cry of the 2nd corps," he wrote to Coleman Leaming. "Our badge is a club and *clubs are trump*."

Ocean Wave's November 19 edition echoed Thompson's praise for the regiment, though in not so colorful language, referring to the 12th's "distinguished" performance in the engagement at Bristoe Station as "brilliant." "The regiment captured as many prisoners as it had men…with few casualties."

Settled in camp, scuttlebutt concerned status of officers. Colonel Willetts, still suffering from wounds he'd received at Chancellorsville, was rumored to be resigning. Thompson's thoughts understandably turned to promotion. As 1863 drew to a close, Thompson was reassigned to the Draft Rendezvous at Trenton because of his public speaking ability and prior recruiting experience. He served in this capacity until May 1864, working to bring the 12th back to full strength.

Meanwhile, the Army of the Potomac welcomed another new commanding officer: Ulysses Grant. Unlike his predecessors, Grant was not reluctant about attacking the enemy, often sending waves of troops against entrenched positions. Thompson observed that such tactics increased the likelihood of men being killed and, quite naturally, voiced a fear that he would be among them.

Grant planned an aggressive campaign on all fronts, with special attention to Richmond. After some intense and inconclusive fighting in the Wilderness, the question in the minds of the rank and file remained: What would Grant do? Would he fall back like the other generals? That same afternoon, the regiment got its answer when Grant ordered the army to move forward. Although they knew more rough days lay ahead, the men of the 12th were pleased.

Thompson, continuing to recruit in Trenton, was promoted to major. With the promotion came orders to return to his regiment. He brought along new soldiers for the badly depleted 12th—transfers from the Reserve Veterans Corps, new recruits and paid substitutes. The former, once known as the Invalid Corps, was a military organization of reserve troops organized to allow partially disabled veterans to perform light duties in the service, freeing up able-bodied troops for the front lines. While perhaps less than perfect soldiers, the newcomers were much needed, even if not especially well regarded.

Grant's war of attrition took a toll, not only on the Rebels but also on front-line Union regiments like the 12th. Lee beat Grant to Spotsylvania, so the Rebels were well placed to greet their adversaries the morning of their arrival. The 12th went into position on the enemy's left. The men moved to cross the Po River, seeking weak spots in the defense.

The regiment initiated a crossing on a recently built pontoon bridge, but before everyone was across, they were attacked.

They returned fire but were outnumbered. Instead of staying, they moved to Spotsylvania, where they faced dense thickets of sharp-pointed cedar posts behind which a hill rose. On top of that hill, a Confederate corps waited, safely ensconced behind breastworks. Despite these formidable obstacles, the 12th attacked. They made it through the cedar barrier, enemy fire notwithstanding. They scurried up the hill, passing extra obstacles in the form of abatis placed across the hillside.

Men snagged on stakes were picked off. Those not shot or skewered rushed back down to the comparative safety of the bottom. A handful remained, stubbornly returning fire until they ran out of ammunition and withdrew. The Federals weren't about to give up. Another attack was planned against a salient in the Confederate line referred to as the Mule Shoe.

Another rainy day and the familiar quagmire in pitch-black darkness greeted the regiment as men made their way hand to shoulder, with the soldier directly in front to keep together. Bayonets fixed, they broke into a double-quick across an open field and up a hillside. Dodging abatis and fallen soldiers, they climbed toward active Rebel rifle pits.

"We sprang on their earthworks yelling and firing like a pack of demons, our guns in their faces," William Haines later wrote. "The smell of powder and brimstone was almost suffocating but on we rushed. At every stop a life was lost…a man went down."

Fighting was close. With sword and bayonet and musket butt, they battered their way through, forcing out the defenders. The 12th pursued, screaming and shooting until they reached a second line of trenches. Rain fell, and the men were soaked through, black with smoke, tired and hungry, but none felt it until it was over. Several officers and sixteen enlisted men were killed or wounded, including Charles Stratton, shot through the skull.

Grant continued advancing south, hoping to draw Lee out from his defenses to fight in the open. By early June, the Federals had reached Cold Harbor—a chance to get at Lee from behind, cutting him off from his supply lines. The 12th reached the bank of Chickahominy River and was ordered closer to the front on the edge of a field, across which the men could see Rebel riflemen. Orders to attack didn't come until the following morning. Crossing the field, they were subjected to fire from several directions. To the veterans of the 12th, it seemed like Pickett's Charge in reverse. The Battle of Cold Harbor, one of the 12th later recalled, was one of the "dreariest, bloodiest, most unsatisfactory of our whole list of battles."

No one from the regiment reached the other side of that field, and there was no help coming from other Union units. The men wanted to retreat, but with enemy fire so hot, most stayed where they were, seeking whatever cover they could find until nightfall, when they escaped. Losses were heavy: fourteen dead and thirty-six wounded, leaving only seventy men available for duty.

The stench of the dead on the killing field grew so unbearable that a temporary truce was arranged to bury the bodies. During this respite, each side experienced the other's humanity. Enemies chatted and laughed together like "we were at a school reunion." Tobacco and coffee were swapped. All too soon, the time was up. "Get down Yanks"—a final friendly warning before it was back to the business of killing.

Grant now focused on taking Petersburg and destroying rail lines connecting that vital supply center to Richmond and the Army of Northern Virginia. Much of the regiment's work at this time involved tearing up rails or guarding others thus engaged.

New troops replenished the depleted regiment. Draftees and substitutes mostly were disdained because they hadn't volunteered for "loftier" reasons like the original men of the regiment. Many were conscripted from reluctant selectees back home or paid by wealthy shirkers taking advantage of a provision of the draft law allowing for paid substitutes. Or worse, they were deserters lured by the prospect of bounty money to reenlist. They were recruited by the man who'd recruited many of the original enlistees, Richard Swain Thompson.

Thompson finally rejoined the regiment on June 23 and, on June 26, wrote to his sister Hannah that he'd met up with an old friend of the family, Court House native Dr. John Wiley, at the 2nd Division Hospital. Wiley was busy tending to the many wounded, particularly new troops experiencing the full effect of Grant's concept of all-out war. Back with his regiment in a week, Thompson received another promotion, to lieutenant colonel.

Thompson-led attacks at Fussell Mill and Bailey's Creek were unsuccessful. Thompson ordered his command to form a charge down the side of a hill, but the orders became confused and the men returned to their original hilltop position, becoming easy targets for enemy fire.

After their effort failed, the entire corps re-crossed the James River. Thompson, as officer of the day, commanded the rear of the withdrawal to expedite a smooth retreat of the last troops to cross. That accomplished, he ordered the dismantling of the pontoon bridge over which they'd crossed. The return march to camp was accompanied by now too familiar Virginia comrades: heavy rain and deep mud.

Reams Station, a depot on Weldon Rail Road, is twelve miles south of Petersburg. The terrain nearby was like that of the Wilderness: thick brush and tangled scrub. Most of the line was already in Union hands, with Lee reduced to using wagon trains to supply his people. But the Federals were determined to destroy the whole line.

Tired from another rain-soaked march and thirsty from intense heat, the 12th further enjoyed the company of voracious mosquitoes and sand fleas. A night camping in mud and continuing downpour did nothing to improve the men's mood.

Assigned to protect a work detail busily destroying tracks, the men willingly pitched in with axe and pick when given a shot at destructive handiwork, doing in three miles before a large body of Rebel troops, infantry and cavalry interrupted them.

Thompson, as lieutenant colonel, was ordered to move his men against the Confederate left. He dispatched five companies to accomplish this. The enemy was reinforced by General A.P. Hill's nine-thousand-man corps, forcing the 12th to withdraw. The bluecoats assumed the defensive against another Rebel attack.

A shell burst in the middle of the gathering regiment, its fragments striking Thompson in the chest, leg and hand, especially his right thumb. Thompson was carried off the field. As Thompson subsequently described it, the thumb "was mashed to pieces against my sword hilt." Nevertheless, he picked up the sword and continued to lead a charge until another shell fragment hit his right side, tearing through his uniform and badly bruising him.

Once under medical care at Emory Hospital, Thompson wrote to his family in Court House, giving more details. "Next day [after being wounded], I was paralyzed in the lower part of my body and both legs. From the center of my stomach wound my right side to back bone was black and blue, eight inches wide besides a cut in the lower stomach." Eventually, the wounded right thumb became so seriously infected that surgeons amputated it. A number of other officers were wounded or captured. Lieutenant James Stratton was killed, another member of that family of brothers and cousins.

The September 11 *Ocean Wave* reported on the battle and Thompson's wound. "Lieutenant-Colonel RS Thompson was severely wounded in making this charge by fragments of a shell, at the same time losing the end of his right thumb."

The regiment retreated toward Petersburg in the aftermath. But its original mission had succeeded. Weldon Railroad was useless to the enemy.

In mid-December, Dr. John Wiley, Thompson family physician, certified Thompson as unfit for field duty, as he required crutches to get around. Richard Swain Thompson's service as a line officer was finished. Once his wounds sufficiently healed and he was able to walk with crutches, the army posted him in Philadelphia, assigned to the General Court Martial for officers. He served as president of the court in Philadelphia until February 1865, when he was discharged from service.

As 1864 drew to a close, Colonel Willetts, long separated from the regiment due to his numerous wounds sustained at Chancellorsville, was finally discharged.

Willets not only survived his wounds but also returned to New Jersey to lead a long and productive life. According to his obituary in the *Bridgeton Evening News*, January 22 edition, he married and established his medical practice at Port Elizabeth, in Cumberland County. Willetts also became involved in local and state politics, serving as a county freeholder, and then he was elected to the New Jersey Assembly for two years, from 1872 to 1873, and finally state senator in 1875.

Willetts also had an odd claim to fame. He knew John Wilkes Booth and frequently engaged in pistol shooting competitions with Booth prior to the war. Washington, D.C., had many shooting galleries where such events were popular.

The 12th began the war with more than 950 volunteers. At the end, 330 reported as "fit for duty," many of these being replacements. The regiment suffered the second-highest casualties among all the New Jersey regiments. Those who survived went back to New Jersey—and peace and quiet.

Andrew Jackson Tomlin

The North Carolina coast from Cape Fear to Cape Hatteras has been called "graveyard of the Atlantic." Near the end of the war, the port of Wilmington, located on the Cape Fear River twenty miles from the coast, was the last commercial connection of the Confederacy with the outside world. Wilmington's inland location rendered it safe from offshore naval bombardment. And the river was some fifty miles wide at its mouth, making blockade impractical.

Blockade-running at Wilmington had caused major headaches for the Union war effort, mostly due to the formidable presence of Fort Fisher, guarding the river entrance. Despite efforts by the Federal navy to blockade the port, runners continued a flow of supplies vital to the survival of Rebel armies.

During a two-month period in late 1864, Wilmington shipped more than 1.5 million bales of cotton to Europe. Cotton was currency for the struggling Confederacy. In return, the port received 8.6 million pounds of meat, 1.5 million pounds of lead, 1.9 million pounds of saltpeter, 550,000 pairs of shoes, 316,000 blankets, 520,000 pounds of coffee and 60,000 rifles. Wilmington represented a lifeline to Europe, particularly Britain. In his book *Confederate Goliath*, Rod Gragg described formidable Fort Fisher. The fort was shaped like the number "7" according to Gragg, with the top line of that numeral stretching about one thousand feet, east–west, across the narrow peninsula on which the fort was situated, while the longer section ran about three thousand feet north–south.

Heavily armed with artillery, Fisher consisted of fifteen traverses, basically sand- and earth-packed mounds rising thirty feet, twenty-five feet thick. These featured hollow interiors that provided shelter for defenders, while the exterior absorbed the pounding. "Bombproofs" connected by interior passageways allowed defenders to pass from one shelter to another unmolested by enemy fire. Attackers would be required to take each traverse one at a time.

The terrain in front of this formidable defense had been cleared for half a mile, affording Rebel gunners an open field of fire. Added to this was a log palisade, running parallel to and fifty feet from the fort wall. It stretched from the river to the ocean—a miniature killing field within the palisade. The wall itself was nine feet high with sharpened points at the top to challenge intrepid climbers. At the angle of the "7" was the Northeast Bastion, towering forty-five feet above the beach. This earthworks tower provided defenders with a perfect view of both approaches.

The sea face of Fort Fisher consisted of another series of twenty-four traverses and gun emplacements extending more than a mile until reaching the Mound Battery. A man-made dune, sixty feet high, the Mound featured two seacoast artillery pieces capable of shelling ships entering New Inlet.

On January 4, 1865, the Union launched a massive attack against this formidable fortress. Commanding Admiral David Porter issued General Order 81, which read in part: "Each vessel will detail as many men as can be spared from the guns as a landing party....That we [the navy] may have a share in the assault, the boats will be kept ready, lowered near the water on the off side of the vessels. Sailors will be armed with cutlasses, well-sharpened, and with revolvers....Marines will form in the rear of the sailors. While soldiers go over the parapets in front, sailors will take the sea face of Fort Fisher....Two thousand men from the fleet will carry the day." One of those marines was Andrew Jackson Tomlin.

When the order signal went out, sailors and marines from thirty-five ships rowed to shore. More than one hundred boats of various sizes were filled with men eagerly anticipating glorious adventure. Hitting the beach under heavy welcoming fire, the initial landing party, armed with shovels, raced to within six hundred yards of the fort and commenced digging trenches. Behind them, marines moved in to occupy the trenches.

The marines advanced, positioning to cover the sailors' assault. They pushed to within two hundred yards of their objective, the sailors falling in behind. The plan then called for marine riflemen to take on Rebels manning the parapets while the seamen rushed the fort. The mission consisted of 1,600 sailors and 350 marines.

The order of attack was very specific as to how the sailors were to behave once inside the fort: "Every three men will seize a prisoner and pitch him over the wall." It had the makings of a swashbuckling Errol Flynn film. Unfortunately, none of the sailors had ever received soldier training. As defenders opened up with grape and canister, sailors mingled disorganized across the beach, presenting clear targets. Each boatload of arriving men behaved like an independent force, following the lead of their particular officers.

The naval bombardment having ceased, Confederates manned the ramparts with everything they had so when the advance commenced, attackers raced pell-mell directly into a reinforced position. Once the attack reached a certain point, torpedoes planted in the beach were set to detonate, isolating the first line of attackers in a perfect spot to be finished off by riflemen.

The Rebels opened fire at eight hundred yards and enjoyed a free firing field, there being no covering fire from the Federals and the ground being completely flat and exposed. There was no place for the sailors to dive for cover. A volley hit the sailors like a flying brick wall. Down they went, killed or wounded, while survivors staggered about in confusion.

Undaunted, the intrepid seamen pressed their disorganized charge, only to be jolted by another volley, a "withering storm" in the words of one survivor. Amazingly, some reached within fifty yards of the fort. Ultimately, the assault disintegrated into a floundering mass of men, desperately seeking cover, while marines struggled to organize counterfire against the fort. Officers tried to rally the men, but in the confusion of the garbled pleas to "charge...don't retreat," many only heard that last word.

In spite of all this, some men advanced but were quickly disposed of by Rebel riflemen. The defenders taunted the hapless sailors as those in the lead fell back. Those advancing from the rear perceived that things weren't going well. Attack became retreat. They turned back as well. Even then, a small group of men pushed forward, only to be pinned down while the bulk of the force raced up the beach in confusion.

The marines maintained a semblance of order, taking cover behind the slope of the beach and returning fire, which afforded some relief to the beleaguered sailors. Rebel fire slackened, enabling a slightly more orderly retreat. Meanwhile, the tide was rising. Holes dug for protection became drowning pools, with the incoming tide indifferently washing over those wounded who couldn't be moved.

At sunset, bodies littered the beach. Cries for water brought out the best in men still trapped on the beach who tried helping those in need. Men risked their lives against persistent rifle fire from the fort to bring those left in the open to comparative safety.

Andrew Jackson Tomlin was one of those who took that risk. His father, John, a prominent farmer and cattle rancher, owned 725 acres in Goshen. He conducted a prosperous produce business supplying hotel kitchens on Cape Island. He built a road from his farm to the resort in order to avoid paying tolls on a new road built a few years before.

Andrew Jackson Tomlin as a young marine. *veteranstributes.org.*

John married Judith Cresse and fathered seventeen children; the sixth was a boy born on March 15, 1845. He named this son after former president Andrew Jackson. Young Andrew attended school in Goshen and worked on the farm until the war started. At age seventeen, he ran away and enlisted, joining the Marine Corps in Philadelphia. Perhaps he'd been inspired by the example of elder brother John, who'd enlisted in the 25th Infantry.

Tomlin would rise to the rank of sergeant. He initially served on the USS *R.R. Cuyler*, performing blockade duty at Wilmington, North Carolina. He transferred to the USS *Wabash*, participating in the attack on Fort Fisher near the end of the war.

As corporal of the guard aboard *Wabash*, Tomlin joined the marine detachment landing with the sailors. Attacking Union forces had been beaten back, their retreat becoming a rout. Tomlin held a position through the night, holding off the enemy until reinforcements finally advanced to the marines' assistance. During this action, one of Tomlin's fellow marines was hit and fell wounded to the beach. Under heavy fire, Tomlin advanced into the open and dragged his fallen comrade to safety in the trench.

Tomlin's marine unit was commanded by Lieutenant Louis Estell Fagan, a Philadelphian not quite twenty-three. Fagan had worked as a clerk before enlisting at age twenty with the 17th Pennsylvania Volunteer Infantry, with whom he served four months.

Fagan reenlisted, this time in the cavalry, the 15th Pennsylvania. He remained on horseback until February 14, 1862, when he received a commission as second lieutenant in the U.S. Marine Corps. The following year, bravery in action earned him a promotion to first lieutenant. His conduct at Fort Fisher would eventually earn him a captaincy.

Commanding his men on the beach before Fort Fisher, Fagan led a dash forward, drawing concentrated fire. He ordered his men to spread out until they reached entrenchments, where they took cover, awaiting the rest of the marines.

In his report of the assault, Fagan wrote, "All my men behaved well but I present especially to your attention, the conduct of Corporal Tomlin of the guard who under a heavy fire of enemy sharpshooters advanced into an open plain close to the fort and assisted a wounded comrade to a place of safety." These words were submitted as Fagan's recommendation that Tomlin be awarded a Medal of Honor.

That award was created during the Civil War. A total of seventeen marines received the medal during that war. Criteria for selection included the need for eyewitnesses, such as Fagan. The act must show conduct "beyond the call of duty" and involve personal risk of life. Tomlin's Medal of Honor citation described his heroic act as "unhesitating" and the enemy fire as "withering." Secretary of the Navy Gideon Welles wrote to Tomlin, complimenting his "gallant and meritorious conduct."

Tomlin remained in the service after the war. He transferred to the USS *Molongo*, which was sent to the Pacific coast, Tomlin continuing on board for about eighteen months. At that point, he returned to Goshen, but not for long. The twenty-one-year-old Tomlin was apparently bitten by the sea bug. He reenlisted in the marines and was dispatched to the Mediterranean aboard the sloop of war *Plymouth*, part of an eleven-vessel fleet. The purpose of this navy presence there was to protect American "interests" while Europe was embroiled in the Franco-Prussian War. During this three-year tour of duty, Tomlin visited the Middle East, where he visited the Church of the Holy Sepulcher, Jerusalem, Bethlehem and other biblical locales.

Tomlin as Cape May County sheriff, one of several political offices he held in Cape May County. *www.cmohs.org*

Finally retired, Tomlin returned to Cape May County, settling on a Goshen farm. He married Sallie Sullivan and fathered a daughter. He was named director of the school in Goshen he'd attended as a boy. Always a staunch Republican, Tomlin was elected to Middle Township Committee and served seventeen years on that body, most of it as chairman. His party tapped him to run for higher office, more or less as a sacrificial lamb against heavily favored incumbent Assemblyman Alvin Hildreth. Despite losing, he tried again, this time for county controller, against another incumbent and another Hildreth, William. Tomlin lost again.

He finally won a countywide election in 1895—a rematch against Alvin Hildreth for sheriff. His election ended what the *New York Times* on October 20, 1895, called "a bitter conflict which threatened to disrupt the party in this county." After retiring as sheriff, he returned to his Goshen farm and a year before his death was named Goshen postmaster.

The November 5, 1905 *Cape May Herald* front page featured a long obituary, complete with artist's rendering of Tomlin, announcing his death "after a brief illness." The lead paragraph noted the "early hour on Wednesday morning, November 1, when Tomlin, age 60, passed across the Dark River….Rising from his sick bed, the Civil War veteran and hero, sat down. His head fell over his shoulder." Attendants understood that the end had come.

The paper concluded by noting that Tomlin's funeral, held in Goshen Methodist Church (now a private residence), was "attended by many persons from all over the country."

CAPE MAY COUNTY COLORED SOLDIERS

Names on gravestones in a cemetery that for the longest time sat forgotten, untended. Names like White, Harmon and Cox. Some names were misspelled. Headstones eventually became overgrown due to neglect. Names like Trice, Wilson and Porter. A few show data. "William Cox died in 1891 at age 81."

Maurice Beesely wrote in his 1857 county history that there were ninety-eight enslaved people in the county according to the 1800 federal census. The county began recording manumissions of its slave population in 1802, according to Rutgers historian Jeffrey Dorwart.

According to William Moore in his article "Early Negro Settlers of Cape May County," "The first black settlers were undoubtedly slaves....Records show that as early as 1664, there were a few slaves who worked with and were treated as members of the family."

Colonial documents such as wills and court records indicate that large landowners owned slaves. John Townsend's "Memorandum Book," kept in the early eighteenth century, describes "two Negro boys belonging to Robert Townsend. Jo aged 18 and Darb aged 13."

The first case of a freed slave in the county occurred in 1790, when John Ware filed suit against an enslaved man named Jethro. Born in the county in 1768, Jethro was bound out by an overseer of the poor to Nathaniel Foster. Jethro had been purchased at birth, and sold several times, before becoming Ware's property in 1788. However, because Jethro's mother was free at the time he was born, the state attorney general granted him freedom.

Bethel Cemetery. *From* Cape May Magazine.

The 1790 census reported 1,150 slaves in the state, 141 of those in Cape May County. Ten years later, the county's total dipped below 100 in a population of just over 3,000. By 1810, records show 191 Black residents among 3,600 residents in total, including 81 slaves. Between 1810 and 1820, slave population in the county declined from 81 to 28. Once the state legislature passed legislation in 1820 affecting the status of slaves, there were zero by 1850.

The 1830 census was the last to list "slave": 3 out of 225 Black residents. According to Dorwart, by 1846, the county's last "slave" was eighty-one-year-old Dorothy Jackson.

Why didn't agricultural Cape May County have more enslaved people? In part, farm economics provided an answer. Most farms in the county were small, so it made more financial sense to hire seasonal help than to keep and house workers. Religion was another reason.

By the nineteenth century, Quakers, constituting a sizable portion of the local population, stopped using slave labor. By midcentury, the Society of Friends had officially come out against slavery. While Baptist churches typically adhered to a policy of strictly separating church from state, First Baptist Church of Cape May Court House in 1841 passed a resolution opposing slavery. The church further declared during the war years, "We are enlisted in our country's service in putting down the rebellion. One of our deacons and a number of our brethren have gone to war."

The *Ocean Wave* of January 8, 1863, printed Lincoln's Emancipation Proclamation, adding editorial comments. "Of its legality and constitutionality, as a war measure, we have not the least doubt but its effects upon the war we are unable to judge."

According to Joseph Leach, the Proclamation guarded against slave insurrection, while being "inspired by the best feelings of humanity, justice, and necessity." Its effects, he added, "should make the rebels aware that slavery was an unsafe situation.…The news will spread like wildfire, even to rebel strongholds where slaves won't initially hear of it." Former Whigs transferred allegiance to the new Republican Party, considered more "radical" on the issue. Many freed slaves remained in the county. According to William Moore, they settled in "clearings in the dense forest. Some intermarried with native Indians who had also been enslaved." The first important Black settlement in the county, Moore wrote, was located near the old Indian trail. Moore listed some of those first settlers: Gibbs, Cox and brothers Edward and Henry Turner. Seasonal employment at nearby Cape Island lured settlers to the area of present-day West Cape May. According to Moore, these settlers included Turners, Coxes and Trustys. In addition to establishing churches, Black communities welcomed itinerant preachers whether male or female to "exhort" at camp meetings. Slaves permitted by owners to attend such meetings were often inspired to seek freedom…both spiritual and literal.

One such exhorter was Jorena Lee. She was born on February 11, 1783, at Cape Island. Her time there with her family was brief. According to her autobiography, she was "parted from my parents at age seven and moved with a Mr. Sharp at the distance of 60 miles from the place of my birth." Lee experienced years of suicidal depression but overcame it with deep religious faith, which inspired her to preach. She became the first approved female preacher in the African Methodist Episcopal Church.

She traveled throughout southern New Jersey, going as far as the eastern shore of Maryland to spread the word. She became familiar with small free Black communities in the region. Her talk about "freedom" often put her at odds with local authorities, especially in slaveholding areas, where she faced arrest. But her words inspired slaves with the idea of "self-emancipation." Among those she motivated was an enslaved Eastern Shore woman named Harriet Tubman.

Left: Jorena Lee, a religious "exhorter" whose words inspired enslaved people to run away. *findagrave.com.*

Right: Harriet Tubman, renowned Underground Railroad conductor, worked at Cape Island. *Harriet Tubman Museum.*

Known for its Underground Railroad activity, Philadelphia became a hot spot for fugitive slave hunters, which may have inspired Tubman to seek out safe havens outside the city. One such haven was a settlement near Cape Island established around 1832. Tubman was familiar with the area, having worked at least one summer at Cape Island. According to Giles Wright of the New Jersey Historical Commission, she was there from 1850 to 1852. While sleepy Cape May County remained relatively isolated from the rest of the country, the country agonized over the slavery question. Voices grew more strident on both sides of the issue. Meanwhile, in Cape May and neighboring Cumberland County, freed slaves established settlements in remote woods and swampy areas. Fugitives from slave states began to join them. One such area was near Cold Spring in Lower Township. As numbers of runaways increased, especially after passage of the Fugitive Slave Act, runaways sought alternate escape routes to those already well established and well known. Town Bank, near Cape Island, was one such depot after crossing the bay.

One case, recorded by William Still, tells of an escape in 1860 during which the fugitives were attacked by white men who tried to steal their boat but were driven off. After rowing through the night, they landed near the "old Cape May lighthouse." They encountered an "oyster boat captain who took them to Philadelphia." Once in the city, they were aided by Still, who arranged their next freedom move to Elmira, New York.

Fugitive slaves escaping from bounty hunters often traveled by boat to reach the county. While it was not considered one of the major routes of the Underground Railroad, boats operating between Lewes and Cape May were known to ferry runaways across Delaware Bay.

In the decade before the war, Cape Island employed numbers of free Blacks. Many worked in the large hotels near the beach, including Congress Hall and Center House. They engaged in considerable give and take on the merits of the institution with visitors from all parts of the country.

Swedish novelist Frederika Bremer described encountering a Unitarian minister from Philadelphia who was "so absorbed by his anti-slavery feelings that his life and mind suffer…he would with the greatest pleasure suffer death if by that means slavery could be abolished." Southern visitors likely would have been happy to accommodate the reverend's wish.

One free Black man, Edward Turner, owned a farm. He also drove a wagon team. It has been suggested that Turner used his farm as temporary hideaway for runaway slaves, while his wagon transported fugitives to remote

Artist's rendering of fugitive slaves fighting with slave catchers in Delaware Bay. *From* Cape May Magazine.

settlements. One route ran from Cold Spring, possibly the Turner farm, to Millville and then to Snow Hill and Haddonfield. If so, he possibly encountered Tubman, who worked at Cape Island for at least one season at the beginning of the 1850s. For obvious reasons, documentation about Tubman is scanty, as are details about the Underground Railroad.

Black residents in southern New Jersey understood that their race made daily living precarious. Slave catchers frequently came into the region and were not particular who they hauled south into bondage. Communication links between free Blacks in the county and slaves of the Upper South, particularly Delaware and Maryland, increased as shipping between the regions increased. Free Black watermen and stevedores secreted slaves aboard northbound vessels.

Historian Joseph Bilby, writing in *New Jersey Civil War Odyssey*, noted that residents of free Black communities "provided refuge for runaways. They armed themselves and guarded their sanctuaries in the event of raids and reprisals by southern slaveholders they had no legal recourse to resist."

Before the war, New Jersey hosted more free Black communities than any other northern state, according to Christopher Barton's "Antebellum African-American Settlement in South Jersey." Quaker communities often had smaller settlements of free Blacks living nearby. Being located in remote rural areas enabled these communities to survive in relative safety, allowing residents to defend themselves in the event of incursions by slave hunters.

Not all the Black residents at Cape Island were service workers. Thomas Dorsey was a successful Philadelphia businessman. He also co-founded the Pennsylvania Anti-Slavery Society. Dorsey owned property at Cape Island, including co-ownership of the Bannaker House, a hotel for Black visitors at the resort, where for eight dollars a week, they could enjoy a seashore vacation—a resort, wrote the *Baltimore Sun*, "for the colored aristocracy."

Dorsey had been enslaved in Maryland until fleeing at age twenty-four. He made it to the Philadelphia home of Robert Purvis, a founder of the American Anti-Slavery Society. In the late 1850s. Dorsey's path crossed with John Brown, in Philadelphia to raise funds for his own antislavery activities. Dorsey helped organize meetings for Brown in the city, including one at Dorsey's home. At that meeting, in October 1859, Brown raised the idea of taking the federal arsenal at Harper's Ferry hoping to incite a slave uprising.

Frederick Douglass was staying at Dorsey's home when news came of Brown's failed effort. Not wanting to be implicated in Brown's plot, Douglass fled to Canada. Dorsey remained in Philadelphia. During the war, he recruited Black troops, especially the 22nd Colored Infantry.

The Bannaker House at Cape Island hosted the Bannaker Institute, an organization devoted to African American culture and promotion of equal rights. An occasional guest was Massachusetts senator Charles Sumner, who suffered a caning on the Senate floor in 1856 during an antislavery speech. Sumner frequented the resort during his recuperation from that injury.

In 1855, Bannaker House issued a "declaration" about slavery: "We lament that the US, though boasting of her liberty and republicanism still hold in slavery $3\frac{1}{2}$ million of our brethren, thus demonstrating to the world its great inconsistency and injustice."

Dorsey's co-owner of Bannaker House was Stephen Smith. Born enslaved in Lancaster County, Smith was purchased by the owner of a lumber company at Columbia, Pennsylvania. Smith worked and saved and bought his freedom at age twenty-one for fifty dollars.

Smith settled in Columbia, a small Susquehanna River town. He developed a successful lumber business while also remaining active in local Underground Railroad activity. Smith owned twenty-two rail cars and canal barges used to carry lumber and coal to Philadelphia or Pittsburgh. They were put to additional use when runaway slaves made their way to Columbia, located near Maryland's border. Adding false ends to rail cars, Smith transported fugitives along with his product. Apparently, slave catchers caught on. Threats of violence became common, as much because Smith was a successful Black man as for his clandestine activities.

He sought refuge at his seaside home while turning his business over to a partner. But Smith remained active, this time in Cape Island real estate. He purchased property near Congress Hall and on Cape Island's more fashionable streets, like Decatur and Jackson. Included in his portfolio was a vacant lot next to his summer home.

The January 2, 1862 *Ocean Wave* recognized Cape Island's illustrious Black seasonal resident, citing Philadelphia newspaper reports about Smith's considerable wealth. "He is most prominent among that city's-colored population and is the wealthiest among them all with a reported worth of $300,000 [$10 million in 2022 dollars]."

Smith branched out in his real estate investments. He joined with William Still to purchase property at Cape May Point, once part of a farm owned by the Whildin family and reputed to be a stopover for runaway slaves. Eventually, the land became site of the Shoreham Hotel, a home for "aged and infirmed colored people."

22ᴺᴰ United States Colored Troops

Headstones record those who survived to come back. Many others who fought in the war and did not return are buried where they fell. Others who survived are buried elsewhere far from the places they'd once called home. Politics—jurisdictional hair-splitting between federal and state governments over which would be responsible. There was also a genuine fear over treatment of Black soldiers captured by the enemy, especially when the Confederacy insisted that Black men captured would be killed or sent into slavery. But mostly, it was prejudice that initially precluded any notion of allowing Black men to fight.

As the war took its toll on Union manpower, the argument assumed a different shape. Passage of the 2ⁿᵈ Confiscation Act of 1862 gave the president authority to use Black soldiers. Lincoln announced Black recruitment in several states. New Jersey was not one of these. Congress followed with the Militia Act, allowing use of Black soldiers "for any war service for which they may be found competent"—including combat.

General Order no. 1 was issued on January 2, 1863, calling for organizing Black soldiers into segregated regiments. Previously, Black men from New Jersey wishing to enlist in the Union army had to travel to New England to join all-Black units like the 54ᵗʰ Massachusetts, which included two dozen Jersey men.

New Jersey resisted recruiting Black soldiers. Governor Joel Parker was pretty clear about his feelings: "Whites should not place their reliance on a distinct inferior race." Nevertheless, more than three thousand Black Jerseyans managed to enlist. Because many Black men left the state to enlist in regiments elsewhere, New Jersey's records of such service are incomplete. This deficiency was exacerbated in the area of identifying soldiers by enlistees' ever-present fear of being identified as a fugitive slave (given that several Union states, such as Delaware and Maryland, still permitted slavery).

An August 1863 *Ocean Wave* article reported that thirty Black men from the county went to Philadelphia to enlist in the "colored regiment." The paper noted that the recruits had a "fair appreciation of the work ahead of them." Other Black residents declared their intention to join as well.

By mid-1863, thirty Black regiments existed, designated U.S. Colored Troops (USCT). Grant felt no hesitation about fighting with the twenty-three USCT regiments assigned to the Army of the Potomac, nor did Ben Butler express any qualms about employing his fifteen Black regiments in the Army of the James.

One of those regiments was the 22nd USCT. The 22nd mustered at Camp William Penn in January 1864 with 681 Jersey men, the most "Jersey" of the USCT companies. Most Black men from the county desiring to enlist did so here.

Camp William Penn was located in Philadelphia, a logical location for a camp for Black soldiers. Local Quakers, having established a record of abolitionist sentiment, were supportive, as was the Union League, which helped recruit troops and financially supported the camp. The city's considerable free Black population was also behind the camp.

Organizing the recruiting effort was a Supervising Committee for the Recruitment of Colored Troops, white men from the Union League. Even so, relations with the local white community were not wholly amicable. And slave owners from nearby Delaware and Maryland caused genuine concern, being ever on the lookout for runaways.

The *Philadelphia Inquirer* described one incident during which soldiers "surrounded a slave owner and threatened him, forcing him to beat a hasty retreat." The *Ocean Wave*'s February 18 1864 edition reported the deaths from illness of two Black recruits from Lower Township at Camp William Penn. "On Saturday last the body of a son of John Murray [Henry] was brought home for internment. On Tuesday, the body of Wallace Trusty was also brought home." Both men had been with their regiment less than five weeks.

Besides health, Black recruits worried about disparity in pay compared with their white counterparts. "When I was home," wrote one soldier, "I could make a living for my wife and my little ones but now I am a soldier and they must do the best they can or starve."

Eleven all-Black regiments trained at Camp William Penn. The 22nd wasn't there very long, heading to Virginia by the end of January. At Yorktown, the regiment built fortifications. The regiment remained there, training and doing manual labor until March, when it supported fellow Jerseyan Judson Kilpatrick's ill-fated cavalry raid on Richmond to liberate Union prisoners of war.

The 22nd marched thirty-three miles to join Kilpatrick's 3,500 cavalry sixteen miles from the Rebel capital. From there, the regiment escorted the raiders back to Yorktown. Their stamina earned praise from at least one officer. "These brave fellows march through mud, cold and rain, some of them almost bare-footed as their shoes were literally torn apart by the thick clay."

Two months later, the 22nd was assigned to an all-Black division in the Army of the James. Grant ordered that army to "threaten" Richmond, drawing troops away from Lee while the Army of the Potomac attacked from the north. The 22nd was issued Springfield muskets, which they used against Rebel skirmishers.

The 22nd faced several thousand men under the command of Major General Fitzhugh Lee. Under a flag of truce, the Rebels suggested that if the Black troops surrendered, they'd be treated as prisoners of war, otherwise they'd be wiped out. The Union men declined, fighting resumed, and Lee's men were turned back. The regiment continued to support the Army of the Potomac into June as Grant moved south from Cold Harbor. The 22nd reached the outskirts of Petersburg on June 15. Company A charged through a ravine, "swept by a storm of leaden hail." Overrunning Rebel trenches at Baylor's Farm, they suffered their first casualties. Newspapers noted the conduct of the Black troops. "Valor of the colored troops—they take no prisoners and leave no wounded," wrote the *Republican Tribune*. Observers especially noted the savagery of the fighting on both sides. To meet its draft quota in 1864, Cape May County enlisted Black soldiers, including Isaac Pepper, Henry Turner and Israel Cox. More than two dozen Black men from the county served, about 10 percent of the county's Black population at the time. Several of the enlistees died at Camp William Penn of illness. This included William Trusty (dysentery) and Jeremiah Smith (typhoid).

The April 14 *Ocean Wave* listed enlistees by township and race, all of whom received $300 from the county as volunteers on the "last day of the enlistment period." Black enlistees from Cape Island included Charles Cox, George Batt, Isaac Pepper, Henry Hawkins and David Trusty. From Lower

Township came Nicholas Bosten, Benjamin Obekiah, Isaac Turner, William Humphries, Lewis Cox, Wallace Trusty, Jeremiah Smith, James Gibbs, Israel Cox, Charles Boss, A. Henry Turner, William Green and Henry Murray.

William Humphries succumbed to typhoid, dying at Fort Magruder, Virginia, in April 1864. Other county Black countians serving included Charles Boze, Jeremiah Smith, Charles Bowles, all privates in Company K, along with William White, a sergeant in Company F. Another sergeant from the county in the 22nd was William Robinson. Smith would serve until he was sent home in March 1864. He died at Cape Island at age twenty. Another enlistee in the 22nd Company K was Benjamin Obekiah. There's some mystery surrounding Obekiah's birthplace. Was it Roanoke, Virginia, or Tuckahoe in Cape May County? One explanation for uncertainty is that escaping slaves with infant children often registered their child's birth in free states.

The 22nd next encountered the "Dimmock Line," a series of earthworks surrounding Petersburg, manned by four thousand enemy soldiers. The regiment took a battery manned with infantry and artillery. At sunset, the 22nd moved to the enemy rear through a gap in the defenses, while other Federal forces attacked the front. In taking the battery, the men exposed themselves to fire. They responded with another charge, this time across a low swampy area and then up an incline. Despite reaching an abatis obstruction, the 22nd dislodged the defenders, but the men were forced to leave eleven dead and forty-three wounded on the field.

After the Petersburg experience, the *West Jersey Press*'s June 29 edition considered the debate about the military value of Black soldiers settled. "A single day's work wiped out a mountain of prejudice and fairly turned the popular current of feeling in this army in favor of the downtrodden race."

Back in Cape May County, the *Ocean Wave* shed some light on one motivation inspiring the aggressiveness of Black soldiers in combat. Its April 21, 1864 edition reported the capture of Fort Pillow by Nathan Bedford Forrest. The Federal garrison was "indiscriminately butchered by rebels who did not spare even children ages 7 or 8....Dead and wounded Negroes were piled in heaps and burned. Out of 600 only 200 remained alive....The negro is a man, a soldier, a hero...never since the beginning of this war saw troops fight better more bravely and with more determination and enthusiasm."

Discussing the issue of Rebel treatment of Black prisoners, the writer offered a sanguine observation: "We can bayonet the enemy to terms on the matter of treating colored soldiers as prisoners sooner than the authorities in Washington can bring him to it by negotiation."

In late September, the 22nd marched toward Richmond, reaching New Market Heights, distracting the enemy from reinforcing Jubal Early and then fighting Sheridan in the Shenandoah Valley. Two assaults failed against strong Confederate positions before the 22nd went in. The Federals finally pushed through to New Market Road. As enemy defenses collapsed, the 22nd led pursuit, taking seventy-four casualties. Cape May's James Gibbs survived this battle and served out his enlistment in the 22nd.

Thomas Morris Chester, Black newspaperman who reported on the 22nd USCT from the front. *www.digitalcollections.org.*

By the end of 1864, the 22nd had been assigned to the 25th Corps, the only all-Black corps in U.S. military history. For the balance of the war, they served in trenches before Richmond. There they were recognized by reporter Thomas Chester as "among the best in the service." Thomas Morris Chester, a Black newspaperman, was unique on the Civil War battlefront.

In December 1864, the 22nd came under the command of a German immigrant, Major General Godfrey Weitzel. A young man in his twenties, Weitzel had previously declined command of Black troops. Now he would command the 25th Corps.

The war's final push came in the spring of 1865. The Rebels finally gave way on April 2 as they fled Richmond. The 22nd entered the city, among the first Union units to do so. Leading his men into Richmond, Weitzel was wary of booby traps, particularly torpedoes and land mines. Instead, the departing Rebels had left other gifts for their adversaries. "Fires and explosions in all directions," Weitzel recalled. "Whites and blacks running to and fro on the streets engaged in pillaging. It was a yelling, howling mob." The 22nd became firefighters and policemen on their first days in Richmond.

Weitzel altered his perception of the Black soldier: "An experiment which has proven a perfect success. Their conduct has been such to draw praise from persons most prejudiced against color." Weitzel backed up his words later, selecting the 22nd to participate in the funeral of the assassinated President Lincoln because of its "excellent discipline and soldierly qualities."

THE DOCTOR

Joseph Smallidge Leach, editor and publisher of the *Ocean Wave*, became the county's voice for modernization and progress, especially the necessity of a railroad. He was political too.

Along with the energetic Dr. John Wiley, Leach helped organize a local Republican Party in the county. Its first cause was promoting the presidential candidacy of Abraham Lincoln. A mover and shaker in the county before the war, Wiley was not a local in the "traditional, *Mayflower* descendant" sense. Born in Salem County, eldest child of a farmer, Wiley attended Jefferson Medical College in Philadelphia, graduating in 1837.

He married into the Hand family (Daniela) and, in 1845, purchased Joseph Fifield's existing medical practice. He also bought his medical predecessor's house both on Main Street, Cape May Court House.

Wiley's wife was a descendant of Shamgar Hand, who originally settled at Romney Plantation, which eventually became the center of Court House. Daniela's parents were Daniel and Esther Hewitt Hand. Her grandfather, also Daniel, in 1764 donated an acre to the county on which the first court house was built, explaining perhaps Wiley's desire to keep the county seat there.

Wiley immersed himself in local community and political affairs. In 1847, citizen factions in Cape May Court House and Dennis Creek vied to determine the location of the county seat. Dennis Creek enjoyed a thriving commercial and shipbuilding economy and wanted to host the county government. Wiley's connection to the long-established Hand family helped

Home of Dr. John Wiley, now a bed-and-breakfast Inn on Route 9 in the heart of Cape May Court House. *From* New Jersey Monthly.

his campaign keep that government where it was. He argued that moving it would entail unnecessary taxpayer expense, always a strong argument with voters. When votes were tallied, Court House was the winner.

Maintaining his medical practice, Wiley dabbled in local banking, which was trying to establish in the county. He joined a venture with Franklin Hand (his wife's uncle) in the Atlantic Bank, which lasted three years until 1851. Undeterred by his less than spectacular success in banking, Wiley became involved with local transportation improvements. The Cape May Turnpike Company sought to extend its existing road into the lower section of the county. Purchasing land along the proposed route, Wiley predicted that there'd soon be "continuous road between Cape Island and Cape May Court House."

His effort was stymied by landowner resistance to selling. Farmers like John Tomlin also objected to paying turnpike tolls to deliver produce from his Goshen farm to Cape Island during the busy summer season. Tomlin turned discontent into action, building a toll-free road alongside the turnpike. This road became known as ShunPike.

Like many prominent citizens of the county before the war, Wiley was a Whig in politics, a supporter of Henry Clay and his philosophies. After that party ceased to exist, Wiley was instrumental in establishing the Republican Party in southern New Jersey. Like many of his fellow new Republicans, he espoused antislavery but was no abolitionist.

The war interrupted Wiley's career and activism. As a middle-aged man at the outbreak, he initially hesitated about volunteering. However, he utilized his organizing skills to arrange a mass meeting at which a "Home Guard" was formed.

Following Union defeat at Bull Run, Wiley volunteered on August 17, 1861, and was commissioned surgeon with the 6th New Jersey Volunteer Infantry, a three-year enlistment. The September 5 *Ocean Wave* announced the event: "Wiley, with whom we have been familiar the last 21 years, left home for Trenton last week to be ready to go to Washington. He is a skillful physician and will no doubt prove an efficient surgeon."

Wiley served with distinction, first as regimental surgeon for the 6th and then advancing to the rank of surgeon-in-chief for the 2nd Brigade New Jersey Volunteers. The *Ocean Wave* trumpeted his promotion: "In addition to the 6th, he will service the 5th, 7th, 8th, and 11th regiments…his promotion is deservedly bestowed." In early November 1861, Wiley wrote to Richard Holmes from camp at Meridian Hill. As with most letter writers, he bemoaned weather conditions, "windy and wet." "The outside of my tent reminds me of the sails of a vessel when she is going about," he observed. Wiley acknowledged his living accommodations were superior to those of the rank and file. "I have a stove and am very comfortable.…Several of the invalid have had to retreat to the hospital tents and, as a consequence, the hospital is very crowded." Otherwise, he pronounced the health of the 6th as "good. All the sick are convalescent, something of a novelty." Wiley closed by informing Holmes that the regiment was about to move closer to the front, "a forty-mile march down in Maryland."

In his three years of service, Wiley was twice cited by superior officers for "going above and beyond." He employed his medical skill on at least one documented occasion "under duress of captivity" after an engagement. An unusually quiet moment in camp was suddenly disturbed by sounds of heavy gunfire. Wiley mounted and galloped off in the direction of an apparent battle, not at all aware of his own troop's position. He wound up behind enemy lines and was captured.

Upon learning that Wiley was a physician, the ever-needy Rebels put him to work in their hospital. They retained him for two months before releasing

Display of Dr. Wiley's tent. (That isn't the good doctor in the tent.) *antiquesscientifica.com/ CivilWar.*

him. The *Ocean Wave* reported his return in its September 25 edition: "He was with the rebels…not taken prisoner however, but voluntarily went with our sick and wounded who had been captured, in order to minister their wants. Magnanimous…as we should expect from him."

The paper noted that Wiley had written to "friends back home" that Federal sick and wounded were treated kindly by the enemy but that the Rebels were "on short allowance," having only one cracker per man a day. "Even these were divided with our sick."

On the day Wiley left to return to Union lines, they'd exhausted their supply of crackers, "leaving them nothing but coffee."

The October 16 *Ocean Wave* published a lengthy article from "Brother Jonathan" who reportedly heard from a Union physician captured by the enemy (Wiley) a detailed description of the "raggedness" of Longstreet's Rebel army, estimating that he'd observed some fifty thousand men at Harper's Ferry. "There never was such a gang of ragged and rowdy-looking men," he reported. "It was like an army of rag-pickers."

There were no uniforms or even "attempts" at uniforms; officers and men were equally dirty. Individual items of clothing were described:

[O]*ld wide-awakes* [hats] *stained by long campaigns, often missing tops. Trousers of various colors and condition, most typically in tatters. Shirts black from long use. Coats dirty and ragged…for those fortunate to possess such luxuries…often "well-greased" by the piece of bacon which each man carried on his bayonet. Crackers were carried in pockets along with bullets and caps…..Nearly half the men were barefoot.…They'd been constantly walking since the battles before Richmond and had had nothing to eat and expressed universal disappointment at their recent reception by the people of Maryland.…These men evidently want both food and rest…a vigorous follow-up of our victory could have easily scattered and demoralized them.*

Unfortunately, the correspondent was not commanding the Union army. The war continued, and John Wiley remained in the thick of things.

An obviously energetic individual, Wiley was also impetuous. According to Dr. Horace Wood II, writing about his grandfather, "Wiley twice had his horse shot out from under him." Wiley's name was mentioned and his conduct praised in official reports written after the Battles of Bull Run and Chancellorsville. He was present for every engagement of the 6th Regiment (and 2nd Brigade after his promotion) from the Siege of Yorktown to the Siege of Petersburg.

At Gettysburg, after tending his wounded following the carnage at Devil's Den, Wiley witnessed the "glorious slaughter of Pickett's charge" from the

Wiley and medical staff of the 6th New Jersey Volunteer Infantry. *Cape May County Museum.*

summit of Little Round Top. Years later, publisher Alfred Cooper recalled Wiley in his memoirs, *My Traditions and Memories*, "The doctor's bravery at Gettysburg was most marked."

His services were much needed during Grant's bloody campaign in Virginia. During the Siege of Petersburg, Wiley wrote to his wife, describing the cat-and-mouse movements of opposing armies before his closing comments: "A heavy rain fell last evening. This morning, I thought they were coming because picket fire was lively in our front at daybreak....I am comfortably fixed under a fly about 50 yards behind our breastworks. In case of battle, shall withdraw farther back to establish a hospital. Love to all. See you soon."

On August 9, 1864, Lieutenant Colonel Stephen Gilkyson of the 6th, reporting the regiment's performance in a recent battle, singled out officers for "special mention for their recent conduct under fire," including surgeon John Wiley. "[H]e labored ministering to the wants of the sick and wounded doing all in his power to alleviate their suffering." That was easier said than done, given the typical conditions of field hospitals—a "swamp of moaning," one correspondent described them. "Men crying for relief. Men lost eyes, teeth, noses, fingers clipped off, had their cheeks hollowed, collarbones shattered, skulls cracked by fast flying lead balls." Discarded body parts piled in corners, to be carted away in wheelbarrows and then fed to pigs. Such were conditions under which small-town physicians like John Wiley functioned.

So, too, did Daniel Whildin Hand, a Court House native (son of Franklin and Daniela Whildin Hand and cousin to Wiley's wife) who studied medicine under Wiley after attending Pennsylvania University. At the start of the war, Hand was living in St. Paul, Minnesota. In 1861, he volunteered his medical skills for the 1st Minnesota Regiment and was promoted surgeon of the U.S. Volunteers.

Following his service during the Peninsula Campaign, Hand worked as medical director in Virginia in 1863 and North Carolina, 1864–65. While at Newbern, North Carolina, Hand faced an outbreak of yellow fever. For his diligence in dealing with emergencies, he was breveted lieutenant colonel.

Hand was wounded at Fair Oaks in 1862 and, the following year, was captured during a skirmish and sent to Libby Prison in Richmond.

The May 28 *Ocean Wave* noted Hand's capture by "roving guerrillas." A more detailed report appeared in the June 4 paper, extracted from the *Philadelphia Inquirer*. Hand had been visiting troops engaged in destroying railroad lines when he was surrounded by armed Rebels. Hand briefly

Daniel Whildin Hand, Wiley's brother-in law and Union medical director during the war. *www.findagrave.com.*

attempted to escape, "[t]hrowing himself on his horse's neck and applying the spurs."

A Rebel bullet pierced the horse's neck, missing Hand. The horse fell dead. Still resisting, Hand was rendered unconscious by a blow from a musket butt. That was the extent of the violence done to the doctor. He was treated in a "gentlemanly fashion" and put on a horse while his captors traveled through swampy land toward the Blackwater. Hand received visits from a number of Rebel officers, recently involved in the Siege of Suffolk. While their conversation was courteous, they insisted that the Northerners should "leave us alone…the Almighty is on our side."

Unmolested and in full retention of his possessions, including money, Hand was put on a train for Richmond. After a brief stay in that city, Hand was released and returned to Fort Monroe. He resumed active duty, serving out the duration of the war.

Wiley was offered the post of division surgeon near the war's conclusion if he remained with the army. He declined. Back home, wife Daniela's health had deteriorated, and he felt that he was more needed there. Completing his three years, Wiley was mustered out on September 7, 1864. Daniela Hand Wiley would live another nine years. After her death, the doctor remarried. Staying in the Hand family, he wed cousin Lydia in 1877.

Wiley resumed his Court House practice and his active involvement in local affairs, finally accepting a nonmilitary government position as Cape May County tax collector.

He also tended to personal business, becoming a landowner and cranberry grower. He tried his hand at banking again as a director of the Mechanics and Laborers Savings and Loan, servicing the county's expanding economic need for local banks. Maintaining his profession over the years, in 1885 Wiley became a founding member of the Cape May County Medical Society. While caring for his dying mother-in-law, Wiley contracted pneumonia and died on Christmas Eve 1891.

Sewell Assumes Command

Mustered on August 19, 1861, the 6th Regiment New Jersey Volunteer Infantry left Camp Olden with 38 officers and 860 noncoms and privates. At Budd's Ferry, Maryland, it joined the 2nd New Jersey Brigade (along with the 5th, 7th and 8th Regiments).

Typical Virginia conditions—incessant rain and muddy roads—combined with lack of sleep and endless toil digging trenches piqued the men's mood to fight. The 6th first experienced combat at Williamsburg in May, after a three-hour slog through muck, the 2nd Brigade holding the front of a line of breastworks at Fort Magruder.

The regiment deployed in woods on the left, enduring hours of heavy enemy fire. Both sides held, exchanging volleys until the Rebels attacked in overwhelming numbers. With ammunition running low, the 6th stubbornly pulled back, but their resistance, in the words of historian John Young Foster, "saved the division from being swept in disaster from the field." Not bad for a first outing.

After this action, Wilmon Whildin, an original enlistee in Company I, was discharged due to disability. While hospitalized near Frederick City, Maryland, Whildin wrote to his hometown newspaper, not about conditions at the hospital but about the "condition" of the local citizenry in that border "slave" state, whom he described as "semi-secessionists."

Far from being ready to abandon the Union, according to Whildin, Marylanders, long thought to be heavily pro-Southern, were "loyal in every sense of the word." He informed readers that locals brought food and

Colonel William Sewell, 5th New Jersey Volunteer Regiment, assumed temporary command of the 6th during Chancellorsville and Gettysburg battles. *New Jersey State Historical Museum.*

clothing to sick and wounded Union soldiers, adding that when General Lee "appeared in that area, expecting the people to rise up in support, he was bitterly disappointed....Aged parents, sunburnt farmers treated him with coolness and indifference....Maryland would not seal her destiny by mingling her fate with the bogus confederacy."

Whildin recovered from his illness. Late in the war, according to Lewis Townsend Stevens's *History of Cape May County*, Whildin reenlisted in a cavalry unit fighting in the Deep South. After the war, Whildin took the path of countless future New Jerseyans, relocating to Florida. In 1898, he was elected West Palm Beach's fourth mayor and was instrumental in changing the town from a shanty "tent city" to a residential community.

At Chancellorsville, the 6th guarded river crossings while fighting raged elsewhere. The regiment was ordered forward, arriving at Chancellorsville on the morning of May 3. Confederates advanced in strong numbers, driving back several Union regiments, while the 6th held its position behind breastworks. At this point, the 6th came temporarily under the command of a man who later figured prominently in the growth of Cape May in the latter part of the nineteenth century: William Sewell.

Sewell was born in County Mayo, Ireland, in 1835. Orphaned during the potato famine, he came to this country at age fifteen. Like many Irish, he initially lived in New York City. There he found work as a merchant seaman. He eventually moved to Camden.

At the start of the war, Sewell raised a volunteer company in Camden for which he was elected captain. This would become the 5th New Jersey Volunteer Regiment. Sewell fought with this regiment during McClellan's Peninsula Campaign, earning advancement to lieutenant colonel in 1862 and, in October, regimental commander.

On the occasions of two major battles, Chancellorsville and Gettysburg, he was called on as senior officer to command the entire 2nd Brigade. At Chancellorsville, Sewell led the 6th, though "terribly thinned" in the fighting, on a charge described by the *Washington Chronicle* as a "splendid achievement." For his conduct, he was brevetted brigadier general for volunteers on March 13, 1865.

During heavy fighting at the Plank Road, he assumed command when General Gershom Mott was severely wounded. Sewell rallied men on the verge of retreating. Instead, they counterattacked. Sewell was wounded, which eventually earned him a Congressional Medal of Honor. "Through several hours of desperate conflict, remaining with his command though wounded, and inspiring his men by his presence and the gallantry of his personal example," reads the citation, awarded thirty-three years after the event.

Sewell recovered from his wounds at Chancellorsville and fought at Gettysburg. On the second day, he led his regiment to reinforce a weakened line near Emmittsburg Road, joining other units charging across a wheat field, driving back the Rebels before reassembling on a "ledge of rocks called the Devil's Den," according to the official report of the battle. The next day, Sewell was again wounded.

But he rejoined his regiment for the Wilderness Campaign. In the early morning of May 6, the 6th entered a break in the Union line and steadily advanced. "Not a man faltered or fell back," John Young Foster wrote, "standing in solid ranks, firing with deliberate aim, they held in check the menacing columns."

Reinforced Rebels counterattacked the left flank and rear, with the Federals adjusting their own lines to meet these maneuvers. Gradually, the Union troops fell back and reformed the line but were again outflanked and forced back grudgingly. Sewell's previous wounds reopened during this action, compelling him to resign his commission.

One might think that he'd sufficiently served the Union cause, but Sewell wasn't finished. As the war neared conclusion, he briefly resumed active duty as colonel leading a recently organized 38th New Jersey Volunteer Infantry.

Sewell received his medal in 1896. A U.S. senator at the time, Sewell had become a major player not only in south Jersey politics but in business as well. A major interest was railroads, specifically the West Jersey and Camden and Atlantic lines. Sewell was a vice-president of the former. He was also director of the Camden and Philadelphia Steamship Ferry Company and controlled considerable holdings in regional banking and insurance companies.

His interests extended to Cape May County, particularly Cape May, where he became involved in resort real estate development. Sewell's Point is located at the entrance to Cold Spring Inlet at the east end of Poverty

Beach—that nickname, an unintended irony given the proximity today of numerous multimillion-dollar seasonal residences. In the mid-nineteenth century, there were no rock wall jetties, no nearby U.S. Coast Guard training facilities and no big money construction. There was an inlet, a powerful tidal creek that shifted with tides and storms.

In 1868, a seafood restaurant was built there, and a road connected the point to the developed area of Cape Island. That same year, Sewell partnered with John Bullitt filling marshland to build the Stockton Hotel. In later years, Sewell joined other group ventures in the southern end of the county. In one, he joined a consortium that included John Wannamaker and Alexander Whildin, founding SeaGrove, which became Cape May Point. By the end of the nineteenth century, a rail line linked Sewell's Point and Cape May Point at the steamboat landing on Delaware Bay. Sewell died on December 27, 1901. He was a U.S. senator at the time.

HENRY SAWYER

He was born Henry Washington Saeger on March 16, 1829, in Egypt, Pennsylvania, third of seven children. Son of Christian Saeger, a farmer, young Henry received little schooling but demonstrated a keen interest in carpentry. At age nineteen, he apparently enraged his father by leaving the farm. Apparently disowned, Henry never laid eyes on his father again.

In 1848, he relocated to Cape Island, where he not only learned carpentry but also worked building the resort's growing hotel and housing stock. He changed his name to Sawyer and married a local girl, Harriet Ware Eldredge. Both sides of Harriet's family had deep roots in the county, being among its original settlers and tracing ancestry back to the *Mayflower*. Harriet's father, Thomas, was married to Deborah Ware. A Whig politically, Thomas fought with the militia in 1812 as a colonel.

When the rebellion began, Sawyer was among the first New Jerseyans to heed Lincoln's call for volunteers. There being no established regimental organizations in the county at the time, he traveled to Trenton to meet with Governor Charles Olden. Unable to join a New Jersey regiment then, Sawyer enrolled in a Pennsylvania regiment. After a month, he was promoted to second sergeant and, less than a month thereafter, to second lieutenant. He was released from service one month later, these Pennsylvania companies being created for only three months. Olden offered Sawyer a commission in one of the newly forming Jersey regiments.

The war's early days was a confusing time in the lower Northern states. Loyalties of those states, including New Jersey, were questionable.

Communications between Washington and Trenton were uncertain, as Southern sympathizers effectively controlled Baltimore.

After Sawyer enlisted in the cavalry, Olden dispatched him to Washington carrying "sensitive" mail to Secretary of War Simon Cameron. Cameron assigned Sawyer to an undermanned force guarding the capital, the 25th Pennsylvania Volunteer Infantry. Eventually, five companies of Pennsylvania troops arrived. Sawyer joined.

The *Ocean Wave* on August 29 reported county men departing for Trenton to join a "mounted company." One of these, Harry Gilmore, wrote to the paper describing his trip to the state capital. He praised Captain Whildin, who "passed them gratis on the steamer *George Washington*." According to Gilmore, "the utmost hilarity and good spirits predominate among the men." They expected to move for Washington before his letter reached Cape Island.

Harry Lake Gilmour (or Gilmore), like Sawyer, was not native to the county. In fact, he was not a native American. Born in Londonderry, Northern Ireland, in 1836, he left home at sixteen, seeking a life at sea. However, when his travels brought him to Philadelphia, he stayed on land. Like Sawyer, he came to Cape Island seeking work in the resort's booming building trades and became a house painter. He joined the 1st New Jersey as a sergeant, but in June 1862, he transferred to the Army General Hospital, where he served as a steward for the war's duration.

After the war, Gilmore returned to New Jersey and trained in dentistry at Wenonah. He also worked as Sunday school superintendent and choir director at his Methodist church. He demonstrated talent for writing gospel songs, putting him in great demand at camp meetings across the region. Gilmore published sixteen books of gospel music during his lifetime.

Sawyer and Gilmore enrolled in Halstead's Cavalry in Trenton. William Halstead was a seventy-year-old Trenton lawyer. Halstead's Cavalry was an independent unit raised under provisions of a July 22, 1861 act of Congress. This particular unit was eventually re-mustered as the 1st New Jersey Volunteer Cavalry.

Olden asked Sawyer to accept a three-month assignment as Halstead's representative to Cameron, while the aged and militarily inexperienced Halstead struggled to organize his regiment. Cameron named Sawyer to a temporary detail guarding the White House, the Cassius Clay Battalion (named for founder, Kentucky abolitionist Cassius Marcellus Clay, Lincoln's ambassador to Russia).

From its beginnings, Halstead's Cavalry lacked any semblance of military discipline. It was large, with more than one thousand men and forty-four officers. The organization's difficulties originated with its founder. Not in the best health, Halstead never garnered the respect his position required.

The *Ocean Wave* followed the regiment's initial difficulties, reporting in its February 27 issue that it was "an independent regiment, not recognized by the governor. Therefore, the men in it are not entitled to state pay." One problem followed another, resulting in Halstead's being court-martialed in Washington for "defrauding the government." He was acquitted but relieved of command.

However, Sawyer's star apparently shone. Rejoining the regiment after Halstead's departure, he advanced to first lieutenant six weeks later. He received his captaincy on October 1. Meanwhile, the War Department engaged a new colonel to command the regiment, a man totally unlike Halstead: Colonel Wyndham.

To fully appreciate the dramatic transformation of farmer/carpenter Henry Saegar into swashbuckling cavalry officer Henry Washington Sawyer, the reader must know Sir Percy Wyndham. Sawyer described his new colonel to folks back home in a letter to the *Ocean Wave*: "An officer of Italian renown, who served as Brigadier General of Cavalry in the Italian army."

Wyndham was not born in Cape May County and never set foot in the county. In fact, Sir Percy was not American. Son of a captain in the British navy, he was born at sea aboard a warship. Wyndham's military career began at age of fifteen when he fought in the 1848 French Revolution that overthrew King Louis Phillippe, ushering in a French republic during that tumultuous year of revolutions that rocked much of Europe.

Wyndham next joined the French navy, attaining the rank of ensign before switching teams and enlisting in the British artillery. The ever-restless Wyndham returned to the European mainland, enlisting in the Austrian army, in which he rose to command a squadron of lancers.

In 1860, he left Austria, heading south to Italy to join Garibaldi's Expedition of the Thousand in Sicily. He received a battlefield promotion to major at the Battle of Millazzo, which opened the way for Garibaldi to Messina and ultimately taking Sicily. For his service, the king of Piedmont, Victor Emmanuel, knighted Wyndham. "He's young—about 30—dashing, and a splendid horseman," Sawyer wrote, "and seems to have all the qualifications necessary for a cavalry officer."

Gilmore wrote to the paper two weeks later, adding his own words of praise for his new commander. "He is a fighting man…he has seen service in the Crimea, at Solferina, and with Garibaldi in the Italian struggle. It is a surety our regiment will acquit itself with honor."

Given Wyndham's penchant for being in the thick of military action, it's no surprise that Sir Percy turned up on this side of the Atlantic at the outbreak of Civil War. He offered his services to General George McClellan. McClellan recommended Wyndham to New Jersey governor Olden, then organizing the state's volunteers, including the badly *dis*organized Halstead's Cavalry.

Sir Percy's appearance likely disconcerted the Jersey men he'd be commanding. He sported a mustache, but what a mustache! Whiskers extended saber-like a full ten inches out from each nostril. The mustache was the most outward manifestation of Wyndham's flamboyant personality. "Colorful," "prissy," "exuberant"—all such adjectives were applied, though never to his face. He affected a foppish manner of walking and was given to wearing hats adorned with flaming red plumes.

The new commander of Sawyer's cavalry was not welcomed with open arms. But the men quickly learned that Sir Percy knew his business and was not to be lightly dismissed as mere peacock. He enacted strict discipline and demonstrated adeptness with the sword, the saber being the weapon of choice for cavalry. Wyndham also scored points by taking care of his men, securing better rations and improving camp living conditions, even regular pay.

Sawyer assured readers back home that the 1st would soon see action. "We are again under marching orders to go with General Heintzman's Expedition…our regiment numbers 500 men where it formerly numbered 1100…we are splendidly armed. Our arms are Burnside's carbine and Colt's army revolver.…Our regiment has done all the reconnoitering, scouting, and picketing for Heintzman's division which was, up to date, the most advanced post of our line…left wing of the Grand Army of the Potomac."

The 1st scouted as far as Occoquam, site of a Rebel fort and battery, situated to prevent the Federals from blockading the Potomac River. The regiment was "ready for action," Sawyer boasted, echoing McClellan's prediction of a "short and bloody conflict." "Treason is commencing to feel our blows…a grand victory of our army will show these rebels that our government is not a government in name but in fact."

Harry Gilmore's April 5 letter to the *Ocean Wave* described scenes he witnessed in these earliest days. "Deserted camps, where some skulls have been found suspended from the ridgepoles of the tents, bearing odious inscriptions, and as evidence of the uncivilized and barbarous character of those black-hearted traitors.…A member of Company E was shown a ring by a woman, purporting to be carved from the bone of a Yankee slain at

Bull Run." Gilmore related how the regiment captured prisoners, a colonel and two surgeons, including "the notorious Dr Nevitt [possibly Napoleon Bonaparte Nevitt, 38th Virginia Artillery]."

The 1st was eager to fight and Sir Percy was itching to lead them. Josiah Granville Leach reported in the paper's May 8 edition on his visit with the regiment at Falmouth, noted Wyndham's recent Washington trip "to see Secretary [Edwin] Stanton." "He told Stanton he did not leave a brigadier generalship in the Italian army to be made a policeman in this country. He said he had a cavalry regiment second to none."

Stanton, according to Leach's account, issued orders granting Wyndham's request, attaching the regiment to General McDowell's division. Sawyer described what happened on the way to Falmouth: "We drove a number of Texan rangers before us…upon arriving at Falmouth we fell in with a band of 1000 rebels, consisting of battery, two squadrons of cavalry and 600 infantry."

Union horsemen advanced and the Rebels hastily retreated, infantry first, cavalry covering, over three bridges. The blue cavalry charged, but the enemy escaped, destroying the bridges behind them. Sawyer bemoaned the unfairness of fighting on the enemy's "home turf." "They have the advantage of us. One beat they are soldiers, the next they are citizens."

He described leading a search of a farm and finding two men, sons of the farmer, their cavalry horses tied up in the stable. He also encountered a beautiful woman, who conversed with Sawyer. "Is this not a sorrowful scene in our southern home?" she complained. Sawyer countered that it was also a "sad sight for our mothers, wives and sisters to see their sons, husbands, and brothers leave home to put down this unholy, unnatural rebellion." He then ordered the girl's brothers taken prisoner. In addition to his letter, Sawyer sent the paper copies of the *Richmond Enquirer*. Editor Leach expressed "amusement to read the huge lies contained in this rebel sheet."

Wyndham's impetuousness often led him into difficulty. In June 1862, Wyndham encountered Turner Ashby, his equally swashbuckling Rebel alter ego. Ashby's cavalry was covering the rear of Jackson's army near Harrisonburg, Virginia. Wyndham was, in his own words, "out to bag Turner Ashby."

The 1st Jersey galloped into an ambush. Undaunted, Wyndham ordered a charge right through combined infantry/cavalry. Greatly outnumbered, the Northerners retreated, leaving Wyndham continuing the advance *alone*. Instead of Ashby, it was Wyndham who was "in the bag." In addition to losing its commanding officer, the 1st Jersey lost more than one hundred horses.

Wyndham wasn't the only bluecoat taken. Sawyer wrote in the local paper's July 3 edition that Harry Gilmour was assisting surgeons tending wounded near Harrisonburg "when the rebels advanced and took the wounded and many others prisoner"—including Gilmour. "When our forces retake Harrisonburg, Mr. Gilmour may get clear," Sawyer wrote. Unfortunately, Gilmour was dispatched to Richmond, where he enjoyed Southern hospitality at Libby Prison for several months.

Wyndham was paroled and rejoined the 1st Jersey, but his penchant for foolhardy gallantry kept causing him difficulties. On another occasion, Sir Percy was ordered to retreat and became so enraged at the disorganized manner with which his troops responded that he ordered them to "wheel back and face the enemy"—this under withering Rebel artillery barrage—all just so they could wheel around in proper formation to execute a "properly ordered withdraw."

"The twirl of that mustache," a characteristic gesture of Wyndham's when angry, was "more formidable than enemy rifles," one trooper quipped.

The July 10, 1862 *Ocean Wave* carried "A Camp Letter" written by Sawyer while the 1st Jersey pursued the enemy toward Richmond. During one scrap with elements of Jackson's army, Sawyer led a charge resulting in the capture of forty-nine prisoners. But hunger presented a tougher adversary for Union troops, according to Sawyer. He described how the men "sucked red clover heads just to get some nourishment."

His regiment tangled with Jackson's army at Cross Keys. Sawyer reported "heavy losses to both sides…Jackson led a masterly retreat." Sawyer joined the pursuit, his horse "jumping over the dead and wounded of the enemy." "I heard the dying shrieks and it made my blood run cold," he wrote. Cold blood or not, Sawyer also informed readers that his conduct earned him an appointment, "provost marshal, rank and pay of captain." Wyndham took a liking to Henry Sawyer, who displayed a bit of dash and daring himself. Within six months, Wyndham promoted Sawyer to first lieutenant and then captain. As captain of Company R, Sawyer led his men on several encounters between October 1862 and the momentous battle at Brandy Station.

Sawyer suffered his first combat wound at Woodcock, Virginia, in 1862. His horse shot out from under him, Sawyer fell, the horse falling dead on top of him. Sawyer's thigh bone was so damaged that for the rest of his life he lived in pain and developed a marked limp.

The July 10 *Ocean Wave* reported Sawyer's homecoming on medical furlough—"[the] first time he has been away from his regiment since they went to war." Sawyer came home bearing souvenirs, captured in Virginia.

"He brought a Colt's six-barrel revolver, taken from rebel Captain Mulligan when he was taken prisoner by Captain Sawyer."

Back with his regiment three weeks later, Sawyer penned a letter in which he called on men of his county to step forward and do their part for the cause. Sounding like a recruiting officer, he cited three reasons for shirking: sympathy with traitors, feigned disability and cowardice. Cape May County, he wrote, "should furnish a company at once…those preferring to serve in old regiments will find a hearty welcome in the 1st Cavalry." Those who are truly unable to serve, he concluded, should aid with "pecuniary means," helping families of those who did enlist.

Sawyer was wounded again on October 31 while leading a reconnaissance near Aldie, Virginia. Sawyer's company encountered 1,500 Rebel cavalry. While covering the Union retreat, Sawyer was shot in the stomach. The bullet lodged near his spine. Army surgeons would not remove it. He laid on his side, almost totally helpless, according to the paper, when he wrote from Seminary Hospital Georgetown, relating that his squadron suffered three killed and five wounded in that encounter. The 1st drove the enemy three miles, he wrote, "receiving fire in front and rear from their cavalry, infantry, and artillery" before retiring "in good order."

Sawyer's wounds, though "serious," were deemed by surgeons "not immediately dangerous." "He suffers much and the surgeon says he will not be fit in less than 60 days." He was sent home to Cape May County, where civilian surgeons were able to remove the bullet. Incredibly, Sawyer returned to duty. The paper reported an office visit from an ambulatory Sawyer, itching to return to action. "His limb is quite stiff yet and the wound is still open."

While the Battle of Brandy Station was a defeat for the North, some historians view it as a significant victory for Union cavalry, when first-time Northern horse soldiers held their own against arguably better led, experienced Southern adversaries. It was the largest cavalry battle ever fought in North America, raging so intensely that friend didn't know foe and units were uncertain which way or whom they were charging.

On June 8, 1863, Lee visited Culpepper, where his celebrated cavalry commander, Brigadier General Jeb Stuart, had arranged a showy review of ten thousand horsemen. Confident in their ability to whip the Yanks, Stuart's cavalry soon crossed the Rappahannock, heading toward Brandy Station. Not sure if Stuart's movement was a feint or vanguard of a larger invasion, Hooker ordered Union cavalry into action.

Brandy Station was a stop along the Orange and Alexandria Railroad, about six miles north of Culpepper. A tavern, Brandy House, preceded the station. Such was the quality of the beverage served that the word was painted on a fence outside the house. When the railroad came through, the word simply became the station name.

An aide to Confederate general Jeb Stuart later opined that Brandy Station "made the federal cavalry." No small compliment, coming from an officer in Lee's vaunted horse regiments, whose previous record had been pretty much perfect. That record had posed serious morale problems for Union cavalry. Were the Rebels that much braver, that superior as horsemen and fighters? In fairness to the men in blue, mitigating factors contributed to the early disparity in performance between the two cavalries.

Union cavalry had not been organized or treated as cohesive units until well into the war. Bits and pieces were dispersed among infantry regiments, with no central command system. That changed when Fightin' Joe Hooker assumed command of Army of the Potomac. Best known for his disastrous performance at Chancellorsville, Hooker rates considerable credit for his efforts to reorganize a disheveled and demoralized army following the Battle of Fredericksburg.

In addition to obtaining his troops better food, clothes and housing, Hooker also reorganized the army, in this case, making the cavalry *the cavalry*—a corps with its own divisions (three). By Brandy Station, its commander was General Alfred Pleasanton. An experienced Indian fighter and veteran of the Mexican-American War, he'd selected capable subordinates, including Brigadier Generals John Buford and David Gregg.

Pleasanton wasn't sure where Stuart was, but Hooker wanted his cavalry to strike at Culpepper. The problem was that Stuart wasn't at Culpepper. The Yankees didn't know it, but as they moved, they headed right into the thick of Stuart's well-placed Rebel cavalry/infantry at Brandy Station.

Gregg's division formed columns and confronted them before the Rebels caught on. In the lead, the 1st Jersey galloped forward into a confused mass of enemies. The Rebels broke, with Jersey men harassing their retreat. Stuart had established his headquarters on one of two rises. Seeing that tempting target, Wyndham formed his men for a charge. The Jersey men, including Sawyer, advanced at a steady trot. Historian Henry Pyne in *History of the 1st New Jersey Cavalry* described their movement: "Wyndham formed the 1st Jersey for a charge. In column of battalions, it advanced with steady trot, its line more accurate than ever on parade…down the steep bank of the cutting and up the other side. A descent and rise of nine feet each way, taken by the whole body without waver or hesitation…so rapid was the advance of the columns that the enemy batteries endeavored in vain to get range on them."

One of those horsemen, Sawyer led his unit crashing into the enemy, scattering them in confusion: "[N]o check to their headlong charge and with dripping sabers and panting steeds emerged into the field beyond." The Southerners had to appreciate the spectacle of it—something out of the pages of their literary favorite, Sir Walter Scott.

Federal forward momentum picked up, moving so quickly that artillery Stuart had placed to protect his headquarters was unable to fix aim. "Dash and flash, conspicuous, showy, knightly" were comments applicable to the conduct of both sides in this encounter. The word *gallantry* was overused in subsequent official reports and memoirs.

Sabers waving, the Federals tore through defenses and captured Stuart's headquarters, the general not being home at the time. Wyndham called up support when the Rebels rallied and counterattacked. Instead of retreating, 1st Jersey charged. Sawyer was among that charge. Their attack scattered the enemy as they rode through the celebrated 12th Virginia and emerged, still in perfect order at the end of the field. "A passage of arms filled with romantic interest and splendor to a degree unequaled by anything our war produced," one Confederate on the scene observed, as the two cavalries collided.

Fighting persisted, the momentum shifting back and forth. Wounded men and horses tumbled to the ground. Soldiers fought hand to hand, saber to saber. At one point, Union men briefly held Fleetwood Hill, assailed by superior enemy numbers. Confederates surged up the hill. Union men slowly gave ground. A dense cloud of dust rose, obscuring the tumultuous and bloody scene.

In the heat of battle, a fellow officer fell. Sawyer rode to his rescue. Meanwhile, the left wing of the regiment attacked a hill containing a second Rebel battery. Their unbroken ranks overwhelmed the cannoneers. Coming up the other side of the hill was a large force of enemy cavalry. The Jersey men held, causing their adversaries to break. But enemy reinforcements were on their way. Would the 1st Jersey falter? Instead, the order was given: "Fours, left about…wheel!"

The 1st Jersey charged. The men made it back to the safety of their lines in good order. But they left a number of dead and wounded on the field. The 1st Jersey lost 56 of 280 men engaged—including Henry Washington Sawyer. "From that day forth, the prestige of the Confederate cavalry was broken," wrote Brigadier General Wesley Merritt, who'd fought in the battle as a captain.

Brandy Station would prove to be the high point in Sir Percy's career with the Union army. He led the fateful charge up Fleetwood Hill, engaged in furious hand-to-hand (sword) combat and, though significantly outnumbered, led several charges that drove the astonished Rebels back. "My entire command behaved nobly," he later reported. "Unmoved by the enemy's artillery fire, when ordered to charge, dashing forward with a spirit and determination that swept all before them." Wyndham suffered a serious leg wound but remained in the saddle and fought until loss of blood compelled him to retire from the field, head held high and mustaches twirling furiously. Sawyer was wounded in two places during the contest for Fleetwood Hill. One bullet passed clear through his thigh. The other struck his right cheek, passing out the back of his neck on the left side of his face. He remained in the saddle until his horse was shot. The beast tossed into the air and fell dead, but not before throwing its rider to the ground, unconscious. Sawyer was left on the field for dead. He revived after the battle and found himself surrounded by dead comrades. He was captured by two Rebel soldiers, who washed the blood from his face with ditch water. He was taken by wagon to Gordonsville. There his wounds were pronounced "mortal."

But once again, Sawyer proved resilient. Able to be moved, he was sent by train to Richmond and Libby Prison. The *Ocean Wave* June 18 edition noted his situation. In his next correspondence to the paper, he reported himself captive. The paper expressed optimism about his imprisonment: "He will be exchanged in a few days, no doubt, and rejoin his regiment." That optimism would prove unfounded.

General John Winder, Confederate provost marshal, utilized vacant Richmond warehouses along the James River as prisons. One of these sites was a three-building complex belonging to Libby and Sons, Ships Chandlers and Grocers. This converted prison was designated for Union officers.

Libby consisted of four rooms, each about 4,500 square feet and provided with a cookstove—not that the poorly fed prisoners had much use for it. More typically, the stove provided meager warmth in otherwise unheated buildings. In any event, most of the food prisoners was issued was typically confiscated by equally underfed guards.

Prisoners were confined to six rooms on the upper two floors. Their facilities lacked beds. There was no protection over the windows. Summers were unbearably hot and winters excruciatingly cold. Not that it mattered. Prisoners were warned to stay away from the windows, and guards were ordered to shoot anyone seen.

Guards' quarters occupied the first floor. The cellar housed slaves and cells used to confine prisoners deemed "incorrigible." Prisoners

Libby Prison, formerly a warehouse. Henry Sawyer's "home" in Richmond. *warfarehistorynetwork.*

endured lack of food, potable water, basic hygiene, lack of clothing and blankets. Problems of disease persisted throughout the war, worsening as the Confederate cause faltered. By 1863, when Sawyer arrived, Libby's population had reached one thousand.

The *Ocean Wave* had expressed itself on treatment of Union prisoners more than a year before and was unsparing in its criticism of the Confederacy. That was *before* conditions dramatically deteriorated. "Federals taken by the rebels are subjected to the taunts and indignities, are scarcely fed and several of our men at Richmond have been shot by rebel sentinels simply for approaching the windows of the prison....The South boasts of its chivalry and generosity and are now showing it," editor Leach sarcastically concluded. The paper would voice greater indignation once Sawyer's story unfolded.

The *New York Times* of November 1863 reported that diseases at Libby included "diarrhea, dysentery, typhoid, pneumonia...the percentage of inmate deaths has increased due to insufficient food, clothing, and shelter." The story sparked outrage throughout the North. The U.S. War Department provisions sent to Libby were redirected to the needy Army of Northern Virginia. Whatever was left over was snatched up by the guards, many of whom had been consigned to living in tents. By 1863, Libby was so overcrowded that prisoners slept spoon-fashion, head to foot, in alternating rows on the floor.

It was to this dismal locale that Sawyer was dispatched after his wounds had sufficiently healed at Culpepper. He wasn't there long before events, previously unfolding elsewhere, profoundly affected his stay at Libby. On April 9, 1863, Union troops arrested Confederate captains William Corbin and T.J. McGraw in Kentucky. Ambrose Burnside, commanding the Department of Ohio, convened a military commission to try the pair. Found guilty, they were convicted of spying. Corbin and McGraw were executed on May 15.

The outraged Confederate government threatened to retaliate. Colonel Robert Ould, Confederate agent for prisoner exchange, informed his Union counterpart, Lieutenant Colonel William Ludlow, that two Union prisoners of equal rank would be executed. A "special order" was sent to Captain Thomas Turner, commandant of Libby, to select two captains from his population to be shot. Turner assembled seventy-five Union captains.

"Gentlemen, it is my painful duty to communicate an order I've received," he pre-ambled before reading the order. He formed the prisoners in a square, the center of which contained a table holding a box. The names of officers were written on slips of paper and placed inside the box. The first two names drawn would receive a dubious honor.

When none of the captains volunteered to perform the drawing, Sawyer suggested U.S. Army chaplain Reverend Joseph Brown, who drew the first name. It was Henry Washington Sawyer. He showed no emotion when his name was called, according to the *Richmond Dispatch*. "Someone had to be drawn and I can stand it as well as anyone else," the paper quoted him.

The reaction of the second "lucky lottery winner" was different. John Flinn, 51st Indiana Infantry, turned white and sagged. Flinn was no weakling however. A Canadian by birth and a Catholic, he enlisted in October 1861 as first lieutenant of his Indiana regiment and in May 1863 was captured in battle at Gaylesville, Alabama.

Flinn asked to see a clergyman. Sawyer wanted to write a letter to his wife. His was not mere sentiment but a shrewdly calculated maneuver. Sawyer believed that if his situation were made known back home, he'd be rescued. His wife and her family had connections to make that happen.

The *Richmond Dispatch* took a keen interest in the case. Its July 7 edition reported that Sawyer "wrote a letter home, reading it aloud to the official observing." "Upon reading the last part," the *Dispatch* reported, "he begged those standing by to excuse him and, turning aside, burst into tears." Even as it screamed for Sawyer's execution, the *Dispatch* stated, "New Jersey should have no cause to be ashamed of his conduct."

The *Ocean Wave* kept abreast of Sawyer's story, reporting July 6 on local activities on the prisoner's behalf. When the news reached the county about his captivity, friends and relatives reached out to Captain Wilmon Whildin, known for "long association with the steamboat interest in this city."

On his own, Whildin traveled to Washington, where he was received by the president and Secretary of War Edwin Stanton. He returned to Philadelphia with their assurance that the government would act "promptly" in the matter. By the time he reached Cape Island, he learned that Mrs. Sawyer had a letter from her husband stating that the Rebel government would allow her and their children to visit Sawyer before he was executed.

Sawyer's letter suggested that his wife "bring Captain Whildin or Uncle WW Ware." Ware was Harriet Sawyer's uncle on her mother's side. Whildin and Ware both enjoyed connections with Congressman John Nixon, one of the few Republican representatives from Democrat-leaning New Jersey.

The Princeton-educated Nixon represented the county in Congress during the war era. His mother, Mary Shaw Thompson, hailed from Dennisville, and the family owned a home there. (It still stands on Route 47 across from Johnson's Pond.) John Thompson Nixon supported both the war and the Lincoln administration, popular positions in his home district.

Sawyer wrote directly to Nixon on November 1, 1863. In his letter, Sawyer rehashed the battle at Brandy Station and his capture, both stories well known to Nixon by this time. He advised Nixon that he was determined to maintain an "unflinching front." "A soldier works not for gain," Sawyer wrote, "glory and the welfare of his country is his aim....I found that pride was what upheld me and was sufficient to nerve me for my fate."

He asked Nixon to intercede on his behalf, to make an exchange. After writing his initial letter, Sawyer and Flinn were confined to Libby's cellar "dungeon." Their new home, more like a vault, measured six feet wide with no ventilation or windows except for a small hole cut in the door. The men were unable to sleep because sentries were ordered to challenge them every thirty minutes, requiring them to reply.

The October 15 *Ocean Wave* reported what a soldier recently released from Libby had written, describing the prisoner's lodgings. "This den which is filthy and horrible is lighted and ventilated only by a hole in the top through which their food is lowered."

The pair wasn't alone in their confinement, having plenty of company in the form of rats. The captives maintained constant watch, battling rats. Attempts to intercede with their captors for better conditions went unheeded, and the day of execution arrived. "We'd almost reached the city [Richmond] limits, when we met a prominent Roman Catholic bishop," Sawyer recalled about the day he was taken to be executed. "Captain Flinn told the bishop he was being executed without rites of clergy. The clergyman, a friend of Jefferson Davis, interceded on Flinn's behalf and obtained a ten day stay for us."

His show of bravado notwithstanding, Sawyer later corresponded with friend, James Stradling, about his initial reactions to pending execution.

The home of Mary Shaw Thompson still stands on Route 47 across from Johnson's Pond in Dennisville. Mary was mother to Congressman John Nixon. *Old School House Museum.*

"Mine Gott Jim, I never felt so weak in all my life as I did when I found I had drawn the 'death prize.'" And later in the letter, he noted, "I was so weak that the tree and the guards seemed to be moving in a circle around me."

Once he became aware of his temporary "reprieve," Sawyer composed his thoughts, asked for writing material and, in the light of a candle, using an "old board" for a desk, wrote to his wife, knowing how long it would take the letter to reach Cape May County and anticipating his wife's immediate reaction.

Letters from Sawyer to friends and relatives at Cape Island, written with the intent of reducing homefront anxiety about the captives' plight, suggested that they were "permitted to purchase provisions and other comforts and these things could reach them through the flag of truce boat by way of City Point."

Harriet Sawyer traveled to Washington, accompanied by Captain Whildin and Congressman Nixon. They met Lincoln on July 14. The president immediately summoned Major General Henry Halleck, then commander of the U.S. Army.

Following executive orders, Halleck contacted Ludlow at Fort Monroe, informing him that the president ordered General W.H.F. Lee and another imprisoned officer be placed under guard in close confinement. Ludlow was instructed to contact his Confederate counterpart, informing him that if Sawyer and Flinn were executed, the two Rebels would meet the same fate. "Retaliation for barbarous violation of the laws of civilized wars," Halleck termed the increased stakes game of stare down.

The July 23 *Ocean Wave* indicated that there was hope for the Union prisoners. "Two rebel officers had been confined, under guard, at Fort Monroe. "The rebels are afraid to begin this wicked and barbarous work of retaliation now that we hold their officers of high rank."

"Rooney" Lee had been wounded twice, coincidentally at the Battle of Brandy Station, a saber cut and a gunshot wound. He was captured by Federal cavalry while recuperating at Hickory Hill, Virginia, at the home of his father-in-law. *Not* coincidentally, from the Union point of view, Rooney was also a son of Robert E. Lee. Rooney Lee was promoted to major general while in captivity.

Rooney was confined to the dungeon at Fort Monroe, joined a day later by the second pawn in the game, Captain Robert H. Tyler. He was not related to former President John Tyler. His wife's family, however, were prominent Virginia landowners. First and Second Bull Run were fought on their property. In addition to farming, Tyler was a teacher before the war. He raised Company C, Virginia Infantry. Like Sawyer, his superiors often described his conduct as "gallant."

After the war, Tyler corresponded with Sawyer. He informed his former adversary that after being released, he returned to the 8th Regiment and was captured a second time. However, his captivity was brief. Three days later, the Army of Northern Virginia surrendered. "My regiment fought the entire war together," he wrote to Sawyer. "I now stand by the old flag, red, white and blue as devotedly as I followed that of the 'Lost Cause.'" In later years, Tyler served two terms in the Virginia General Assembly and was a trustee for Manassas School for Colored Youth.

Lincoln's gambit paid off. The paper reported that the executions had been "stayed by the prompt actions of the government." It also noted that Mrs. Sawyer, having traveled south, had been refused permission to proceed from City Point to visit her husband at Libby. "The breach of promise is shameless and refusal to allow her to visit is heartless," the paper fumed. The

Rebs' reason? "Confederates had been denied similar visitation privileges to the North to check on relatives or property."

The execution date for the Union officers passed. They remained in their luxury accommodations until August 16, when they were reunited with fellow prisoners. Meanwhile, as Sawyer hoped and Lincoln anticipated, their plight became a major media sensation in New Jersey. Newspapers called for their release and decried the shabby treatment Mrs. Sawyer received in the "gracious" South after she was not permitted to visit her condemned husband. "Evidence of the atrocious vindictiveness on the part of rebel leaders," the *American Standard* of Jersey City complained. The *Richmond Examiner* fired back: "When the Yankees conduct themselves like Christians with us, they may expect a like return." That paper continued clamoring for the prisoners to be executed, but cooler heads prevailed.

At the end of 1863, Lee and Tyler were moved to Fort Lafayette in New York Harbor. In February 1864, the Confederates proposed a swap: Lee and Tyler for Sawyer and Flinn.

Time passed excruciatingly slowly at Libby Prison, as reflected in Henry Sawyer's January 18, 1864 letter to the *Ocean Wave*. "At night, when I lay upon my hard couch and nothing is to be heard but sentinels calling every half hour 'All's well' the thought arises frequently—how will I spend tomorrow?…The morning light does not bring with it gladness but only to usher in another day of uncertainty and misery."

No news came about his status. No indication of a truce. Thoughts of again seeing "friends, family, and flag" kept him going. But lack of news about the rumored prisoner exchange "extinguishes the spark of life yet left." He wrote of other men losing the will to live because of their precarious situations at Libby. They died in prison and were buried in unmarked graves. "Perhaps he leaves a wife…children may depend upon him for succor," Sawyer wrote, "it is doubtful if his family will ever know what became of him."

Since Rooney was a general and a Lee, and the Yanks mere captains, the Southerners threw in a Union general, Brigadier General Neal Dow. Rooney was traded for Dow, while Tyler was swapped for Sawyer and Flinn. Dow, former governor of Maine and outspoken proponent for temperance, was the highest-ranking Union officer in captivity.

On March 14, Henry Sawyer walked out of Libby Prison, a free man. A week later, Sawyer's old commanding officer, Sir Percy Wyndham, recommended Sawyer's promotion to major. Sawyer received that commission at the statehouse from Governor Joel Parker.

The March 23, 1864 *Philadelphia Inquirer* reported Sawyer's homecoming. "Captain Sawyer, a prisoner at Libby Prison for nine months arrived in this city on Monday. Being the last 40 days without meat, is of course somewhat weak but he is in good spirits and hopes to rejoin his regiment at an early date."

The *Ocean Wave* subsequently reported the county's exertions to honor Sawyer, noting that he "was involved in raising funds for the Sanitary Commission in Philadelphia."

The U.S. Sanitary Commission was civilian-run, sanctioned by the federal government to advise the military on mental and physical health of the troops, assist at hospitals and camps and help transport the wounded. The commission provided food, clothing and medical supplies in situations when the military came up short. The organization received no government money, relying on donations and fundraising to do its work. Hence the importance of having men like Henry Sawyer promoting its efforts.

Locals quickly acted to arrange an event honoring him before he resumed those duties. "Handbills were posted Friday night and Saturday morning, music and refreshments organized in a whirl of activity." On May 20, residents of Cape Island recognized Sawyer at an affair held at the Methodist church. Church choirs sang. S.R. Magonagle, now owner of the *Ocean Wave*, made a speech honoring Sawyer.

According to local historian Bob Elwell, writing in the February 2, 2011 *Cape May Star and Wave* (a "descendant" of the *Ocean Wave*), a rousing rendition of "America" was followed by prayer and presentation to Sawyer: "a complete set of cavalry gear, saddle and bridle."

While the crowd admired the gift, the choir broke into a refrain of "Rally Round the Flag Boys" before the evening's honoree regaled his fans with accounts of the Battle of Brandy Station and his sojourn at Libby Prison, although by then everyone had memorized the details of both.

The saddle outfit came in handy because Sawyer's military career was far from over. After furlough recuperating with family at Cape Island, Sawyer returned to the 1ˢᵗ Jersey. He fought in the Battle of Kingston, Virginia, receiving two more wounds, minor.

At the conclusion of hostilities, Sawyer was breveted lieutenant colonel, a rank he held when his regiment was officially discharged. Before exiting the service, Sawyer was offered a lieutenancy in the regular army, which he declined. His final assignment brought him to cavalry headquarters in Washington, where he was employed as a horse inspector, a position he held until he was honorably discharged.

Riding with the 1st Jersey, Sawyer received seven battlefield wounds, three life-threatening. He carried a musket ball in his body for the rest of his life. He also dealt with bouts of typhoid fever and dyspepsia. Sawyer and Gilmour weren't the only Cape May County men to fight with the 1st New Jersey. Sawyer's brother-in-law, William Brooks Eldredge, youngest son of Thomas and Deborah, served initially as a private in Company D after enlisting on August 13, 1861. He transferred to Company K just before Brandy Station, survived that battle and completed his service on September 16, 1864. Returning to Cape May, Eldredge became assistant lighthouse keeper at Cape May Point.

John Warner enlisted in August 1861 as a first sergeant. The *New York Times*' September 8 1862 edition listed Warner among the "sick and wounded transferred from Washington DC Hospital to Portsmouth Grove, Rhode Island." Warner not only survived his condition, but he also reenlisted on January 1, 1864.

The *Ocean Wave* noted his return to the county on leave in its April 7, 1864 edition. "He looks well and has borne himself manfully in many hard-fought combats." Warner returned to combat duty before he was discharged on July 24, 1865. Just before being discharged, he was promoted to second lieutenant of Company D.

And what of Sir Percy? Wyndham not only survived the war but also continued his global military exploits in Asia, primarily India and Burma. He met his end in Rangoon. According to the *London Times*, he died not of wounds earned in glorious combat but from playing with balloons. Intending to soar to the heavens in a balloon of his own design and construction, Wyndham rose five hundred feet, only to have his balloon burst, casting him into a nearby lake, killing him on impact.

9ᵗʰ Regiment

David Burch, Samuel Corson, Josiah Craig and Enoch Hand enlisted as privates on September 20, 1861, in Company C, 9ᵗʰ Regiment, New Jersey Volunteer Infantry. Their three-year terms commenced when they mustered at Camp Olden at Trenton.

They wore distinctive uniforms: dark-blue tunics and sky-blue pantaloons featuring green trim. While spiffy uniforms added inducement for recruitment, the Cape May boys enlisted because the 9ᵗʰ was promoted as an elite organization.

Job Heritage and Richard Heritage joined them, drilling in basics of soldiering until December, when the 9ᵗʰ's 1,037 men shipped to Washington. The 9ᵗʰ was armed with Model 1861 Springfield rifles, weapons with bull's-eye accuracy up to five hundred yards. That helped earn the regiment its unique designation. According to "The Jerseymen and The Plow Boys" by Gilbert Riddle, the 9ᵗʰ was termed a "rifle regiment," men considered the best shots the state had to offer. The ranks also included "watermen" from Bayshore counties like Jeremiah Garrison, a shipbuilder at Goshen before the war. This combination would serve well, given the nature of the war they'd fight.

The *Ocean Wave* newspaper extolled the county boys in the regiment. "Volunteers…worthy representatives of Cape May loyalty."

The 9ᵗʰ headed for Annapolis by train in a snowstorm on January 4, 1862. It joined the fifteen-thousand-strong Burnside Expedition bound for Fort Monroe, North Carolina. The expedition arrived in mid-month at Hatteras

Reuben Hunt Leaming, private, 9th New Jersey Volunteer Infantry, nineteen years old when he enlisted. *www.findagrave.com.*

Inlet, where winter weather was not welcoming. Gales greeted the Northerners, wrecking several vessels. Troops were sardined in a "hole of a ship along with 600 others during a raging storm."

A narrow strait separated Pamlico and Albemarle Sounds. In the center of that strait sat Roanoke Island, twelve miles long by three miles wide. Treacherous channels paralleled the island. Roanoke was a strategic point commanding access between the sounds.

The 9th was first to land, glad to be ashore. It was healthier to face Rebel guns than churning sea. Nestled between Nags Head and the mainland along the two-hundred-mile Outer Banks barrier island chain, Roanoke offered a logical spot for defenders to concentrate forces. And it was the logical place for Burnside to attack first. Should that island fall into Union hands, the Confederacy would lose a rail link to Virginia, jeopardizing supplies and communications for the Army of Northern Virginia.

Reuben Hunt Leaming. Samuel Hearon. Horace Platts. All were from Cape May County and landed on Roanoke Island on February 8 following a fierce artillery duel between Union gunboats and enemy shore batteries. Upon landing, the attackers engaged not only Rebels but also dense swamp. They advanced until they reached Rebel fortifications.

The *Ocean Wave* reported that the regiment "participat[ed] in the principal assault on the enemy's main territory during which they waded through mud and water up to their waists." Cannon fire proved especially troublesome for advancing Federals. Sharpshooters were tasked with taking out the cannoneers. They accomplished this with alacrity. Their marksmanship was described as "remarkable, given that the shooters could see only heads above the works," while exposed to return fire.

Ammunition ran low, but the 9th's commander ordered the regiment forward: "Charge 9th. Charge." Not a memorable quote, but it roused the men. Negotiating assorted swamps and man-made obstacles, the regiment broke through and defenders skedaddled, leaving behind a grisly scene. "As we entered the works, the sight presented was one I never desire to witness again," recalled Josiah Craig. "Men lay dead, others in agony of death with blood streaming from their wounds. The road down which they retreated was strewn with blankets, drawers, shoes stockings, hats, knapsacks, guns and axes." That episode earned the men a reputation that accompanied them throughout the war: the "Jersey Riflemen."

Charles Miller Preston, who would rise to the rank of sergeant, was there, along with Daniel Cosgrove and Corporal Jeremiah Crowell. All fought with the 9th in North Carolina. "After our victory," Craig wrote home, "we were put on the double-quick in full pursuit and after pursuing them five miles we came upon them in a large field, white flag flying."

Driven from their fortifications, the defenders surrendered. According to John Young Foster, Federals took 33 artillery pieces and 2,800 prisoners. Not a bad start. The regiment suffered casualties: 9 killed and 25 wounded. Roanoke Island was now in Union hands.

Among the killed and wounded was Job Heritage of Green Creek. Heritage lived as a boy on Cape Island, the paper noted. The March 7 *Ocean Wave* further praised the 9th's action. "While the Army of the Potomac struggled in the main theater, the taking of Roanoke Island was a bright spot for supporters of the Union cause made more especially gratifying given the performance of the Jersey Blues, the muskrats of the 9th."

Back home, Unionists celebrated the regiment's accomplishments. The local paper described it: "On Friday the 14th, patriotic citizens of Court House fired a national salute." They used a cannon that hadn't seen duty since the War of 1812. They waved a flag sewn by "some fair ladies," including "Aunt Sallie Hand," age eighty-six and mother of the county clerk. Aunt Sallie's claim to fame, according to the paper, was that as a "bright-eyed maiden" of twelve years, she strewed "aromatic flowers" in the path of George Washington as he crossed a bridge at Trenton.

Burnside ordered "Roanoke Island, February 8, 1862" added to the regimental banner. The 9th remained until March 11 before sailing to the mouth of the Neuse River. Because they'd performed so ably in negotiating swamps, the 9th acquired another nickname: "Jersey muskrats."

Reuben Chester and James V. Clark, other Cape May County men, endured the 9th's eighteen-mile march to New Bern. During the march, the regiment engaged Rebels successfully on several occasions, the accuracy of the sharpshooters taking deadly effect each time.

Upon reaching their destination, they encountered entrenched works extending from the Neuse across the rail line to an "impenetrable swamp with strongly armed forts on either flank…sweetened with heavy rebel gun and artillery fire." What to do in the face of such obstacles? The 9th charged. "Leaping from ditch to ditch. Wading knee deep in mire. Rushing around pits and man-made abatis," the irresistible assailants swept over the earthworks, climbing their blood-stained slippery sides before capturing the entire line of fortifications in their front. New Bern quickly became a Union town.

The regiment lost sixty-two killed or wounded during the affair. Among its captured trophies was a South Carolina regimental flag. "Bravo for the Jersey Blues," the *New York Tribune* trumpeted.

After its exertions, the regiment "rested in camp." Their diet consisted of dried beef or pork, desiccated (dehydrated) vegetables and the inevitable hardtack (thick cracker-like bread difficult to chew and even harder to swallow) and coffee. Hardtack arrived in boxes marked "BC." The men, engaging in that timeless tradition of making fun of army food, suggested that rather than Bureau of Commissary, the letters denoted the historic period when the stuff was produced.

Corporal Edward Pullen, one of the county's "muskrats," was promoted to sergeant on February 1, 1862, and first sergeant one month later, based on his performance during recent battles. He served out his three-year enlistment, achieving the rank of first lieutenant.

Writing home on May 28, Josiah Craig described the "Bloody Ninth" looking "hearty and quite healthy, losing only two men to illness" at New Bern, described as "quite a business place" after the Yanks rebuilt its recently destroyed bridge.

Having enjoyed a Thanksgiving feast of "Bogue Sound beef," the 9th joined another force sent to destroy a railroad junction at Goldsborough, so-called headquarters for the Confederate Department of North Carolina. The *Ocean Wave* ran a lengthy correspondence from the regiment, dated December 12, describing the 9th "[f]ording creeks to assault enemy batteries, making their way through waist deep swamp, rebuilding sabotaged bridges… no matter what obstacles they confronted, the Jersey boys overcame."

The writer described the action: "[A]lmost immediately after commencing our new advance we came upon a force of the enemy and entered upon a heavy engagement.…After sustaining a terrible fire from the enemy. The 9th obtained a position close to the bridge and then found ourselves on the banks of the Neuse with a long fortification on the other side."

The Union advance drew within two miles of Kingston by mid-December, when they again met resistance. Both sides raced for a bridge the Rebels had not yet burned. The Confederates won the race and torched the span. The *Ocean Wave* continued to exult in the heroics of the 9th. "Among our regiments, none have won richer laurels than the 9th in North Carolina," Joseph Leach wrote. There was more praise from Congressman John

Nixon. "One out of eight of her [county] people stand on the ranks of the Union Army....The words 'Roanoke' and 'New Bern' on the banners of our gallant 9th are an earnest of what her other regiments will accomplish. The people of Cape May County feel that all this generation should perish than that our experiment of free government should fail." Returning to camp at New Bern on December 20, the regiment's main adversaries seemed to be "alligators, mosquitoes 'big as roaches,' quicksand and bushwhackers." The latter were locals who professed loyalty—by day— only to turn terrorist by night, attacking Union pickets and performing assorted "mischief."

The Yanks encountered something else they hadn't been trained to deal with: increasing numbers of fugitive slaves seeking help from the Northern invaders. The runaways needed food and shelter in addition to protection from vengeful masters. "We gave them houses to live in, plenty to eat, and put them to work for the government," one soldier recalled. That "work" included felling trees used to build, among other things, a hospital. Women cooked, washed and mended clothes for their "protectors." Runaways were paid a small wage for their labor. Exulting in newfound freedom, they frequently entertained the troops with music and "comic dancing." A veteran of Company K observed, "They seemed to be intelligent men and women...laboring under many inconveniences." For many Yankees, including the farm boys of Cape May County, this was their first interaction with the formerly enslaved.

For his part in the 9th's military actions, First Sergeant Edward Pullen was promoted to first lieutenant on December 23.

Goshen's Garrison family was well represented in the 9th. It was informally known as Garrison Town, according to maps showing the Middle Township land where the Garrison family lived since moving to the county in the 1830s. One of those properties was owned by Jeremiah Garrison of Company C of the 9th. Before the war, he married a Goshen cousin, Mary Ann Garrison, with whom he would have fifteen children.

Jeremiah served until the end of the war. Afterward, he returned to New Jersey and became a shipbuilder for a few years before relocating to Sangamon County, Illinois, like many others from the county in the nineteenth century. Brother Robert, who served in the 38th Regiment New Jersey Volunteers, accompanied him.

This county exodus to Illinois started during the national financial panic of 1839. That year, twenty county families formed a wagon train near West Creek and headed west.

Benjamin Garrison, a three-year enlistee, died of typhoid at 3rd Division Hospital in Greensboro, North Carolina. A fourth Garrison brother, John, enlisted in March 1865, serving four months.

The 9th began 1863 with fewer than four hundred men ready for duty. One private from Cape May County, Enoch Willetts Hand, was not with the regiment in the new year. His hometown newspaper reported that he'd been "wounded in the head in a recent North Carolina engagement." Fortunately, the paper reported that the wound for this son of Charles Hand of Court House was "not serious." He eventually returned to complete his three-year service.

The depleted 9th was included in a reorganized brigade of veterans designated the Star Brigade. Unlike other units, this special group shuffled about to various theaters for the rest of the war, dispatched wherever there was greatest need. Moorhead City was one such place. The regiment headed there on January 20 aboard two troop ships, destined for Charleston. With the men on board for a week, under stifling conditions, the weather abetted their misery by storming until January 31, when they finally entered Port Royal Harbor, forty miles south of Charleston.

The *Ocean Wave* reported on the move from North to South Carolina, adding that on January 2, the 9th received a late Christmas gift: "The standard from the state in remembrance of Roanoke and New Bern....We have no fears of hearing anything but favorable reports of the conduct of the 9th...wherever they go."

Eager to go ashore, the men instead were confined to cramped quarters for another ten days, while expedition commanders argued over who would command after landing. Once ashore, there was more waiting, while the navy collected the ships necessary to attack heavily fortified Charleston.

Jersey veterans encountered Black soldiers wearing blue uniforms for the first time. Their reviews were mixed. Some grumbled that it was an "insult to brave soldiers," while others suggested that Black volunteers would become good soldiers, given the chance.

Racial prejudice was not unique to the men of the 9th, many of whom, especially the Cape May County boys, had limited contact with Black people, whether slave or free. But the men were especially vocal in voicing opinions of these soldiers in uniform. The prevailing consensus seemed to be that they were "undisciplined and skittish under fire."

The regiment also encountered a different kind of Black Southerner in this area of South Carolina: those who'd already acquired a degree of independence. Those of the Sea Islands had forged full-scale communities before the war. Charleston slave owners routinely left their workers in charge of their properties during summer months. (Many of these Southerners were familiar with Cape Island, where they sought refuge from summer heat and malarial conditions prevailing on the islands.) The absence of white overseers encouraged liberated attitudes among the island slaves. The Union capture of Port Royal in 1861 chased most of the area's planters away for the duration of the war.

Friction developed between local Black residents and Union troops, many of whom were taken aback by what one termed their "saucy attitudes." Unpleasantness ensued. On one occasion, fifty native homes were burned following an altercation.

The reaction of General David Hunter, commanding the Department of the South, displeased many of the men of the 9th. Hunter was a known abolitionist and early advocate of military service for liberated slaves. Because no one admitted setting the fires, he denied the entire regiment fresh bread and beef for a month. Drills were increased, as were roll calls. No one was permitted to leave camp without written authorization. The men, complained one soldier, "were treated not as Union volunteers but as Union prisoners."

Even without Hunter's restrictions, life in camp weighed heavily. Boredom led to increased feelings of lassitude, reflected in numbers of soldiers turning up for sick call. Others became belligerent, causing breakdowns in discipline. It even affected the sharpshooters' acclaimed marksmanship. More target practice helped there—at least the men could get out frustrations blasting away at imagined enemies, including perhaps an unpopular general.

The 9th eventually put out to sea, coming to anchor on April 5 in the North Edisto River, eighteen miles from Charleston. On board their transports, men listened to the thunder of the cannons. But they couldn't see that most of the damage occurred against their own vessels, sunk or knocked out of commission by formidable defenses constructed by Charleston's commanding general, P.T. Beauregard. None of the Federal ships drew in close enough to inflict much damage. Charleston remained in enemy hands.

On April 10, the 9th returned to Port Royal. There it learned that it was being sent "home" to North Carolina. In the words of one soldier, the men "let out a loud cheer," happy to depart from Hunter, who "never gave the 9th a chance to do anything."

While the 9th traveled slowly to North Carolina. Lieutenant General James Longstreet assumed command of Rebels in the North Carolina theater.

Under him was the equally accomplished D.H. Hill, the latter installed at Goldsborough. Hill's initial objective was to retake New Bern with a siege force of nine thousand seasoned veterans.

The Federals double-quicked twenty-five miles to reach the site, only to find the enemy had vanished. The regiment camped at New Bern, guarding one of the state's dwindling numbers of functioning rail lines. This duty assumed greater importance given Lee's interest in retaking New Bern and that vital supply line.

Meanwhile, the Jersey men received back pay, always welcome, especially to needy families regularly checking the mail back home. They also acquired new uniforms, courtesy of the New Jersey patriots. While camped at New Bern, they learned about draft riots in New York City. As with the issue of arming the formerly enslaved, opinions were mixed concerning the riots. However, a majority felt that rioters should be "shot down." Perhaps the Jersey Rifle regiment could be shipped north to perform that very task? The draft riots raised a different question in the minds of tired veterans: how to get reliable recruits. One answer was to dispatch north a nine-man team of recruiting "agents" that included Edward Pullen.

With three-year enlistments expiring, efforts were taken to re-sign veterans. If three-fourths of a regiment reenlisted, those signing were granted thirty-day furloughs to go home. Those opting to complete their term were assigned to other companies. The reenlistees were known as Veteran Volunteers. Bonus money proved a major factor encouraging reenlistments.

The effort worked with the men of the 9th, the only New Jersey regiment to attain Veteran Volunteer status. According to John Young Foster, two-thirds of the men in the regiment signed up for "another three years of the war."

David Burch was appointed corporal in December 1864. He'd be promoted to sergeant six months later. Sam Corson and Augustus Spalding reenlisted too. Benjamin Heritage joined them two days later. While those boys went home to visit family and friends, others in the 9th who decided to serve out their original enlistments were sent to Deep Creek to fight until their time was up.

Recovering its original strength, the regiment joined a large Union force at Portsmouth, from which they sailed to advance on Williamsburg. Hoping to keep the enemy off-balance, the Federals switched methods of movement several times, from land to water, before finally reaching Bermuda Hundred on the south side of the James River. While the 9th was maneuvering, the Army of the Potomac emerged from the Wilderness.

The movements of the 9th toward Petersburg coordinated with those of the Army of the Potomac, crucial to Grant's strategy to squeeze the Rebels and their principal cities.

The morning of May 14 dawned with the roar of artillery as the 9th fought its way to Fort Darling. The Jersey sharpshooters shone on this occasion, picking off enemy cannoneers with such success that Rebel artillery was rendered inoperative. But the enemy held the fort.

On May 16, under cover of dense fog, Rebels left that stronghold to attack, encountering the line of the 9th. They came within five paces of the Federals, bayonets fixed. The 9th fired a deadly point-blank volley, but the Southerners persisted. A second volley was released, and again they faltered but pressed the attack, coming at the flank. But the Union men had repositioned to meet the attack with another concerted fire. Finally, the 9th gave way after suffering heavy casualties—about 150 killed and wounded.

The *Richmond Examiner*, crowing over the Jersey Riflemen's setback on May 19, backhandedly complimented the 9th's record. "The celebrated New Jersey Rifle regiment has been completely destroyed—thus ridding the bleeding Carolinas of a terrible scourge." Battered, yes. Destroyed? Hardly.

The 9th was next shifted to a different front, reinforcing the Army of the Potomac as it headed into Cold Harbor. When the 9th was ordered there on June 3, it was the first combat experience for Jeremiah Garrison, who'd joined the regiment one month earlier. Brother Ben had recently succumbed to typhoid.

Arriving after a morning battle in which the Federals lost seven thousand men, the 9th dug in despite intense enemy fire. In many cases, digging was accomplished with pocket knives and coffee cups serving as shovels in the hands of desperate men, who simultaneously resisted enemy onslaughts, which persisted until darkness intervened. Such fighting continued for the next seven days until Grant moved to Lee's right. The 9th was assigned to cover the movement before returning to North Carolina, having sampled the war the Army of the Potomac had been fighting. Their uniforms reduced to shreds, they reached New Bern in time to face a more formidable foe than the Army of Northern Virginia: an outbreak of yellow fever. Several soldiers of the 9th died; many more were bedridden. More than one hundred men were more fortunate, as their enlistments expired and they left camp for home. Among them was Corporal Enoch Willetts Hand, Company C. Color bearer for his company, Hand left service on a positive note, a letter from regimental commander Colonel James Stewart recognizing Hand for his conduct during the Battles of New Bern and Goldsborough, where he was wounded.

Other county boys who reenlisted were staying to finish out the war. Among this group was First Lieutenant Edward Pullen. After the commanding officer of Company C was killed at Drury's Bluff, promotions were made from within the ranks. On September 9, Pullen was promoted to captain of Company H.

The 9th was shifted to the right flank at Petersburg in late June and was immediately subjected to heavy enemy artillery fire and infantry attacks. The men beat the attacks back repeatedly before being moved back to a safer position. Such movements became a pattern throughout the siege summer. Units regularly rotated from the busy and deadly front to rear positions in order to more equally share the danger.

At times, trench life became so stressful that some men resorted to shooting off their trigger fingers, rendering them unfit for combat. There is no record of any Cape May County men taking this drastic measure. An exceptionally hot Virginia summer added to the overall strain and weariness. Combined with frequent torrential downpours, conditions were perfect for a proliferation of insects. Conditions became so bad that whenever a man raised his head above a trench, in addition to Rebel bullets, he likely encountered swarms of mosquitoes and gnats.

While building fortifications during the Petersburg stalemate, the regiment learned of still another change. The regiment was ordered back to North Carolina, which it reached during another downpour. The men didn't seem to mind a little rain.

New recruits joined the regiment, and there was talk of politics, national elections distracting from the tedium of camp life. The men of the 9th favored Lincoln's reelection, believing that it represented the best way of ensuring victory on the field. But they felt cheated because they had no say in the matter. Democrat-controlled New Jersey denied the vote to soldiers in the field. Among those soldiers whose states *did* permit them to vote, the incumbent won by a four-to-one margin.

The adventures of the 9th continued on December 5, as the regiment again shipped out to Plymouth near the mouth of Roanoke River on Albemarle Sound—old stomping grounds for the Jersey men. They engaged Confederates in several clashes, which included a familiar enemy tactic: bridge burning. Undeterred, Union soldiers became bridge rebuilders, which they used to cross over, toward Williamsburg.

The advance continued the following week, distracting Confederate forces in North Carolina, while major operations continued elsewhere. Their activity featured long marches without shoes, blankets or coats. The climax of the campaign occurred in February 1865 with the 9th re-securing Roanoke Island.

After they finally reached Goldsborough, the town promptly surrendered. The Federal flag and colors of the regiment flew over the Goldsborough courthouse. Their timing was fortuitous because advance troops of William Tecumseh Sherman arrived next day. They shared news all had been anxiously praying for: Richmond and Petersburg had fallen. A few days later brought even more welcome news: Lee had surrendered.

Sergeant Charles Miller Preston lived in South Seaville after the war. His grandfather was a colonel in the Revolutionary War. *Dennis Township Old School House Museum.*

On June 14, 1865, 216 men of the 9th, enlistments expired, turned in their rifles and mustered out. Those returning to Cape May County included Captain Edward S. Pullen, Corporal Reuben Hunt Leaming, Sam Corson, Charles Preston and Sam Hearon.

William Burch, an original enlistee, wasn't with them because he'd been discharged on March 17, 1863, after being wounded in action at St. Helena Island.

Charles Preston came home to South Seaville, married Elvira Voss, daughter of John Voss and Amy Van Gilder Voss, and built a house on Main Street. Joining Preston on the trip north were two of the Garrison brothers, Jeremiah and John.

One month later, Augustus Spaulding joined his former comrades, settling back to normal life in Cape May County.

25TH REGIMENT

New Jersey resisted drafting men to serve in "Lincoln's army" after the August 4, 1862 order to the state for eleven regiments of 10,478 men to serve nine months. These would become the 21st through 31st Regiments. Since these were short-termers, the original plan was to use these new troops in auxiliary roles such as garrisoning and protecting supply and communication lines. It didn't work out that way for the 25th.

The state struggled to meet its quota through enlistments, even with a rush to join before September 3, the start date for the draft. Amelia Hand described the county's mood about the draft in her diary. "The first of September was when drafting was to begin. But Cape May County was determined to raise her quota by volunteers."

The quota for Middle Township was fifty-nine. One month prior, Dr. Coleman Leaming and Amelia's brother, Franklin, initiated a recruitment drive. The first week netted twenty-one volunteers. By the deadline, Middle's quota was filled. "The evening of August 29, Middle Township Volunteers took supper at Court House and at eight o'clock started for Millville," Amelia wrote.

"At the call of a bleeding country," the *Ocean Wave* enthused, "our young and middle-aged men, with the fire of patriotism burning within, tear themselves away from the endearments of home leaving behind affectionate parents, wives, children and sweethearts to face a rebel foe that they may act in maintaining the constitution of the supremacy of the best of laws."

A similar rousing scene ensued at Cold Spring Academy, where volunteers from Lower Township and Cape Island boarded carriages that conveyed them to Millville on the first leg of their quest, but not before stopping at Dennisville for a hearty supper provided by citizens of that community.

They were joined next day by Middle volunteers. Gathering at Millville, they were regaled with a "sumptuous" breakfast and serenaded by Millville Brass Band while they dined. The band then escorted their heroes to the train station, where recruits boarded cars bound for Camp Beverly.

Bonus money fueled enlistments. The County Board of Freeholders authorized payments of fifty dollars per enlistee. The 25th Regiment was officered and equipped before the deadline arrived, with Companies F,G, and I composed mostly of Cape May County men, mustered on September 26.

John Goff, first sergeant, Company F, 25th New Jersey Volunteer Infantry. Goff came from a long line of Eldora Goffs, one of the earliest families to settle that area. *Dennis Township Old School House Museum.*

The occupations of Company F varied. Most were farmers (forty) or laborers (thirty-three). Other trades were also represented: two artists, eight carpenters, nine seamen, a pair of printers, two clerks and a shoemaker. The shoemaker, Captain David Blenkow from South Seaville, was put in charge. Company F consisted of men mostly from Dennis and Lower Townships.

Blenkow was an immigrant, born in Edinburgh, Scotland, who relocated to Dennis Township at an early age. He enlisted on September 5, was elected by the men and commissioned captain three weeks later at Camp Beverly. Blenkow would lead Company F until the Battle of Fredericksburg, after which he resigned in January 1863.

The 25th's first lieutenant, also elected, was Nicholas Godfrey, an Upper Township man. He described the early days of the regiment in his diary. Godfrey noted Blenkow's election as captain after the "Dennis Township men" arrived at camp, with himself voted in as first lieutenant. Four days later, selections were made "official" along with Henry Young Willetts as second lieutenant. Godfrey also described the regiment's early days. "On

David Blenkow, captain, 25ᵗʰ Regiment, Company F, stands before his home in South Seaville. The home still stands and is a private residence. *Dennis Township Old School House Museum.*

August 29, left home for war and arrived at Millville about four next morning. On August 30, we reached Beverly at noon and was sworn into the service of the United States. This morning [August 31], we find ourselves in the big brick church at Beverly and among 150 men and many are sick with measles."

Company G hailed in large part from Upper Township, especially around Tuckahoe. It was captained by Charles Powell, a blacksmith by trade.

Three-fourths of Company I hailed from different parts of the county and was commanded by John Tomlin, a Goshen farmer. Tomlin would be promoted to captain on March 20, 1863.

That company's second lieutenant was another farmer, Samuel Eldridge Douglass. Douglass's family roots in the county extended deep on both sides, with family names with pre-colonial antecedents like Hand, Eldridge and Douglass. The Dias Creek native would finish his stint with the 25th as first lieutenant. He subsequently reenlisted as sergeant major with the 38th Regiment near the end of the war.

Company I's sergeant was John Spalding. Not native to Cape May, Spalding was born in Philadelphia. After the war, he resided in the county, where he served as a justice of the peace. Spalding's son, Augustus, also a Union soldier, served with the 9th New Jersey. Both survived the war.

Most of the men of Company I were either farmers (thirty-six) or seamen (thirty-seven). One of the latter was Freeling Hewitt, a merchant seaman. A private in the army, "civilian" Hewitt became a captain, commanding a lighthouse for nearly forty-five years.

When Hewitt assumed that position in 1874, he became the first permanent resident

Nicholas Godfrey, first lieutenant, 25th Regiment, from Upper Township. He stayed with the regiment until after the Battle of Fredericksburg, after which he resigned. *Upper Township Historical Society.*

of Anglesea, its lighthouse overlooking the treacherous Hereford Inlet. This was a time when the only access to the barrier island was by boat.

During his years on the island, Hewitt married. He and his wife, as well as their two daughters, lived at the lighthouse. His second daughter was born there in 1886. His older daughter, Lena, was married in a ceremony at the lighthouse. Hewitt might have remained on that job until he died, but at age seventy-five, he was required to retire. He died eight years later in 1927.

Another seaman who'd survive army service was James Chester, from Eldora. Chester's father was a sea captain in coastal trades for more than thirty-five years, shipping cordwood down the Atlantic seaboard. It was assumed that James would follow in his footsteps. That career path was interrupted when the younger Chester enlisted in Company I. Chester fought at Fredericksburg and Suffolk and, though not a landsman, came through on his feet.

John Young Foster, in *New Jersey and the Rebellion*, described the men of the state's 25th Infantry Regiment as a "snapshot" of the state's diverse population. "Streetwise city boys from Paterson mixed with farm boys from

Hereford Inlet Lighthouse in Anglesea, where former 25ᵗʰ Regiment private Freeling Hewitt served as light keeper for nearly half a century. *Hereford Inlet Lighthouse Museum.*

the southern end of the state. A significant number of the latter hailed from Cape May County," wrote Foster.

The regiment officially mustered on September 26 and drew uniforms, which Godfrey was assigned to distribute. The regiment received marching orders on October 9. A heavy guard surrounded the camp to discourage last-minute mind changers.

The *Cape May Ocean Wave* reported the 25ᵗʰ's first "military activities" at camp. "We were all, 44 in number, drawn up in line of battle," the correspondent reported. "Sworn by General [George] Robeson. A medical inspection over, quarters were provided in an unfinished brick church… our rations were drawn consisting of salt junk, bread, molasses, coffee, and potatoes. Having had no sleep of any amount for two nights, we slept at the rate of 40 knots without rocking."

The next morning, more than one newbie awoke with achy bones, little realizing that the previous night would be the most comfortable sleep they'd enjoy for the next nine months. "Dear Wave," a correspondent wrote, "We are progressing in the school of the soldier…no arms have been given us as yet. But when they do come, won't we honor our loved country and sustain the Union of our birth."

141

The 25th left New Jersey on October 10, 1862. "This morning we left Beverly for the seat of war [Washington]," Godfrey wrote. "It commenced raining about the time we started. We arrived in the city [Philadelphia] about 4 o'clock and had a delicious supper and seen [*sic*] many of our friends from the cape."

They ate at the Union and Cooper Shop. "Might be the last decent meal we would partake of for a long day." The next day, the 25th was in Baltimore. It was still raining, and the men were unceremoniously deposited on that city's muddy streets. A crosstown tramp brought them to their next train. The men, many of whom had never been outside New Jersey, had already seen "many different scenes through the night, passing over steam boats and long bridges...already a long way from home."

But at least they didn't encounter problems with Baltimoreans. "The streets were empty, no mob traitors," the correspondent noted, referring to earlier incidents of violence between Southern sympathizers and Union troops passing through. He assured readers that the 25th had "barrels ready to deal with trouble."

The journey's last leg was "the worst." The train crawled forty miles with constant stoppages, during which the men were fed "'soldiers' crackers and salt horse." Those who managed to catch a few winks did so while "packed like sardines." They arrived in Washington on Sunday, October 12. Godfrey was less than impressed. "It is quite cold and disagreeable." Godfrey wrote. So was their reception.

They marched unceremoniously from the train depot to makeshift camp on Capitol Hill, east of town. There they were assigned to Sibley tents—twenty men to a tent. "We pitched our tents in the mud." This was an experience with which the Jersey boys would become quite familiar.

Drill, dress parade and endless reviews between, with a bit of D.C. sightseeing squeezed in—that was Nicholas Godfrey's initial Washington experience. Then a familiar face from home turned up on October 20 when Dr. John Wiley visited the Cape May County boys in camp, Godfrey recorded.

Henry Willets and Reuben Foster visited Alexandria, Virginia, to visit friends stationed in the 7th Regiment. Godfrey made the trip the following day. His journal mostly complained about weather. "Windy to the point of raising the very earth...everything in camp is covered."

October 25 was a big day. The 25th was issued arms at the Washington Arsenal. The men exchanged old weapons, "some marked 43 BC as the date of construction," quipped correspondent Josiah Leach. Leach was exaggerating for his readers, but the men felt like they'd been short-changed, not by the current administration in Washington but rather by Lincoln's predecessors.

Private Firman Willis was interviewed by the *Ocean City News* in 1930. Ocean City's "only Civil War veteran" still resented James Buchanan as secretary of war and later president, a "southern sympathizer." By diverting arms to southern arsenals prior to the war, Buchanan had left the North "crippled," forcing the War Department to purchase whatever inferior weapons it could obtain.

Fortunately, Willis added, "We had much better guns later on…mine was an Enfield rifle." "We were delighted with the change as our pieces were lighter and of better quality. We hoped to do some good execution with them when the powder, ball, and blood arrived."

Godfrey recorded visiting fellow countian Jerome Bowker at Cliffburn Hospital. Unlike many of his comrades, Bowker survived his hospital stay and completed his enlistment with the nine-month regiment. October ended as it began: guard duty and drill and foul weather. Complaints about weather and living conditions were familiar reading in the hometown newspaper. "Thick dust" rendered the "grub unfit for anyone but soldiers to masticate." "It rained hard all night [October 25] and in the morning the mud was ankle deep…it has been cold and I have rheumatism bad," Godfrey wrote.

When the regimental camp relocated from Capitol Hill to the south side of the Potomac at the end of October, Godfrey was laid up with that rheumatism. When the 25th received marching orders, he was left behind to move baggage and the sick.

Health problems persisted among the men. Nearly every soldier fought colds. Members of Company F were hospitalized with assorted ailments, with measles, diphtheria and rheumatism being the most common complaints. One member of Company F who contracted scarlet fever was John Woolson Reeves. The fourth son of Joshua Reeves, John had gone to work at age thirteen after his father suffered a stroke. He was one of four brothers to serve the Union cause (as well as a cousin Abijah Reeves and two brothers-in-law, Daniel Crowell and Sergeant Albert Stevens Edmunds, all of the 25th).

In addition, another Reeves, Uncle Abraham, a state assemblyman at the war's outbreak, raised a company and led it to volunteer at Camp Beverly in 1862. While some of those men eventually enlisted, Abraham was turned away due to his age. He was sixty at the time. During the war,

"Uncle Abe" continued to contribute to the Union cause through his involvement with the Christian Commission.

John Reeves was discharged for disability on February 14, 1863, and returned to the county. He took up farming. Reeves's ambition extended beyond agriculture. He went into shipbuilding. He owned several vessels involved in coastal trade, transporting gravel. Additionally, he held interests in local real estate and banking. Reeves turned his attention to politics as well. A staunch Republican, he was elected to Lower Township Committee, as county freeholder and as county sheriff.

John Woolson Reeves, one of several Reeves brothers and assorted extended family members to fight for the Union. After the war, he was elected Cape May County sheriff. *Encyclopedia of Prominent South Jersey Citizens.*

In early November, the regiment was in Virginia at Fairfax Seminary (now Arlington National Cemetery), described by the *Ocean Wave* as "confiscated property of the famous rebel, General Lee." The 25th performed picket duty until the end of that month, at which time, marching orders came through.

The "picket house," readers learned, was used to watch enemy activity along the front. The paper described the structure as "rails, cedar and pine boughs piled on three sides to form a shelter with the front open." The men's initial experience with picket detail featured a heavy snowstorm, during which they performed what became common chores: building breastworks and digging entrenchments.

Godfrey's diary stuck to weather complaints, describing their first weeks as "cold and blustry [*sic*] and stormy." Snow also accompanied the regiment on its eighty-mile march to Aquia Creek on December 8. By then, diarist Godfrey was back in the hospital, suffering high fever. He'd "fainted away" after taking an emetic. He subsequently recorded that fellow countian Thomas Beckwith had succumbed to measles in the hospital.

Ordered out of camp on November 30, soldiers prepared seven days' rations of pork and biscuit, which they packed along with small shelter tents. The latter, *Ocean Wave* correspondent Leach lamented, "provided little more than imaginary covering" against seemingly perpetual Virginia rain.

The regiment crossed the Potomac on pontoon bridges, joining the main army at its Falmouth camp, assigned to the 9th Corps, 1st Brigade,

The *Daily Wave* newspaper office in Cape May. Since its inception, the paper has undergone a number of ownership and name changes. It's still published today as the *Cape May Star and Wave*.

3rd Division. Meanwhile, their commander, Ambrose Burnside, planned an attack on Fredericksburg.

Activities of the 25th were regularly reported to the *Ocean Wave* by fellow soldier Josiah Granville Leach, son of the paper's publisher. Leach served as chronicler, submitting weekly dispatches from the war.

His father, Joseph Smallidge Leach, was something of a Renaissance man—ordained minister, schoolteacher, local government official, newspaper writer, editor and publisher. Leach arrived at Cape Island in 1848 from New England. He became deacon at Cape Island Baptist Church, a post he held for forty-three years. He taught school in Lower Township as well.

In 1851, when Cape Island incorporated from borough to city, Leach was elected first recorder for the new city council. Busy Leach was also justice of the peace. He found time to father eight more children during all this activity.

The county's first newspaper, a four-page weekly, began publication in June 1855. Three months later, Leach bought the paper. From this new "pulpit," Leach advocated what he believed were the best interests of the county. In particular, a railroad line, the Cape May and Millville, was his preference.

With the onset of war, Leach employed his journalistic energy promoting the Union cause, both in the paper and at public rallies, where he demonstrated considerable gifts for public speaking.

In 1863, Leach added Cape Island postmaster to his lengthening résumé. He also served as superintendent of Cape Island Schools and was elected to the County Board of Freeholders, all in 1863. The latter office enabled him to push for financial support from the county for area soldiers and their families.

Son Granville was writing for the paper at the outbreak of war. When Granville enlisted in the 25th as a sergeant, he became the *Ocean Wave*'s "war correspondent." But young Leach also had a warrior's heart and sincere belief in the Union cause. "Emotions of a heart that throbs in unison with every word written and it's God's will and must be carried out to a successful issue."

Leach's December 11 piece for the paper was reported from the battle front as the 25th formed opposite the city of Fredericksburg. Upon reaching the south bank under heavy enemy fire, the regiment set pickets along the streets of Fredericksburg. The pickets were led by Corporal Joseph Garrison from Cold Spring.

After experiencing the horrors of war, Garrison's postwar life led him to the clergy. His ministry extended fifty-nine years until his death in Philadelphia in 1931 (at age ninety-three). Another countian, Leaming Weatherby, shared picket duty.

The pickets remained until the morning of December 13. The Jersey boys made the most of their temporary respite in town, "lounging around in the mansions in rocking chairs and sofas, drumming away on pianos and enjoying quite a jubilee with confiscated tobacco." That is, until the bugle called them to arms. They moved to a point from which they watched the already raging battle. "We could see the troops march gallantly upon the enemy, on the charge. And down fell hundreds to rise no more," Leach wrote.

Joseph Garrison, corporal, 25th Regiment. After the war, he pursued a different calling— fifty-nine years in the ministry. He died at age ninety-three. *www.findagrave.com.*

The regiment was designated to attack fortified and artillery strengthened Rebel positions in the woods and on hills overlooking Fredericksburg. Shelby Foote described that setting as a "natural amphitheater revealed to sunshine as the early morning fog lifted."

After initial efforts by other companies ended disastrously, the 25ᵗʰ advanced, having witnessed considerable slaughter among their fellow Union soldiers. Their attack route led across an open field, exposed to enemy fire, reaching a stone wall, behind which Confederate infantry waited, supported by artillery.

The enemy concentrated a killing fire on the field. It would have been understandable if the newcomers balked at the suicidal assignment, but they didn't. Taking the center of a reformed attack line, the 25ᵗʰ charged straight toward the entrenched enemy, attacking uphill, across the field, an ideal shooting gallery for short-range, concentrated rifle fire.

Leach recalled dropping his haversack to lighten his load before joining the charge. Federals surged forward "double quick," maintaining a semblance of ordered line, pushing through ravine, over fences, crossing some eight hundred death-filled yards to within fifty paces of the enemy. There, they were finally compelled to halt.

The scene was incredibly noisy. Shrieks from men falling, wounded and dying. Deafening screams of other men summoning the courage to move ahead. The booming shock of cannons, trembling the very earth, shells landing among prostrate men. The nonstop crack of musketry.

As darkness fell, casualties mounted. Finally, the regiment withdrew, returning to the point from which it had started. Nine men were killed and another fifty-eight wounded.

The dead sprawled in "every conceivable position," a Union soldier assigned to burial detail described the aftermath. "Some on their backs with gaping jaws, some with eyes as large as walnuts protruding with a glassy stare, some doubled up like a contortionist. Everywhere horrible expressions…fear, rage, madness…lying in pools of blood half buried in the mud…a fragment of shell sticking in oozing brain, bullet holes all over puffed bodies."

The night after the bloodletting, nature put on a special show in tribute to the dead, the aurora borealis, seldom viewed this far south. When nighttime temperature dropped below freezing, many of the wounded still lying on the field gradually froze to death. The lightshow didn't mean much to them.

The battered 25ᵗʰ finally retired, reforming what was left of the line before making an orderly retreat, with Companies A and F last to withdraw, according to Leach. They moved behind a high embankment, regrouped and returned to Fredericksburg. Two days later, the Army of the Potomac re-crossed the Rappahannock and reentered its old camp.

For his valor, Leach was promoted to sergeant major and eventually second lieutenant, a rank he held for the duration of his enlistment. After the war, Leach briefly returned to Cape Island, where he worked for S.R. Magonagle, then owner of the *Ocean Wave*. Leach relocated to Philadelphia and graduated from law school, entering the Philadelphia bar in 1866. He helped organize relief for victims of the Johnstown Flood.

He served in the Pennsylvania legislature before becoming appraiser for the Port of Philadelphia. However, he retained his Cape May County roots, marrying Elizabeth Whildin, daughter of steamboat operator Wilmon Whildin. Leach organized aid societies for sick and disabled veterans. In 1880, he was commissioned commissary general for the Pennsylvania National Guard. He never forgot his time serving with the 25th or lost his devotion to the Union. At his urging, in 1893, citizens began the practice of displaying the flag on June 14, now an annual event, Flag Day.

Busy as he was, he found time to author numerous books of family histories—curiously no Cape May County *Mayflower* families—and was a founder of the Genealogical Society of Pennsylvania. While he maintained a summer residence in Cape May, he died at his Chestnut Street home in center city on May 27, 1922.

The Pennsylvania Society of Sons of the Revolution

Colonel Josiah Granville Leach

JULY 27th, 1842   MAY 27th, 1922

A FOUNDER

A PRESIDENT

AND AT THE TIME OF HIS DEATH,

HONOURARY PRESIDENT

ORIGINATOR OF FLAG DAY JUNE 14th.

Proclamation honoring a man of many talents. Josiah Granville Leach was a newspaperman, attorney, legislator and genealogist. The citation notes his role in creating what has become an annual national event, Flag Day. *Cape May County Museum.*

For some officers of the 25th, the carnage of Fredericksburg proved sufficient to remove any romantic notions about war. One member of the regiment described the assault as a "lumbering attack against impregnable works." "It can hardly be in human nature for men to show more valor," a newspaperman reported. "Or for generals to manifest less judgment."

Nicholas Willetts Godfrey resigned as first lieutenant after the Battle of Fredericksburg. He was replaced by Henry Willets. Godfrey did well for himself after the war. He relocated to Long Island, where he farmed salt hay and asparagus. He was also an inventor. According to the *New York Times'* October 10, 1899 obituary, he was credited with the first steam-powered sand shovel, used to excavate sand mines. Godfrey eventually became a major landowner, developing much of Long Island, where he'd settled.

After completing *his* nine months enlistment with the 25th, Henry Willets came home and worked for the U.S. Life-Saving Service. Assigned to the station at Townsend's Inlet, then an unpopulated barrier island, Willets served until 1876, when he died in line of duty.

Sergeant Reuben Foster advanced to fill Willets's former rank when Willets replaced Godfrey. Foster had been farming in Iowa prior to the war but returned to the county to enlist. His bravery during the Fredericksburg Campaign earned him promotion, a rank he'd fill until the end of the 25th's enlistment.

Foster came from a long line of Cape May Fosters. His namesake grandfather was ruling elder of Cold Spring Presbyterian Church for forty-four years. His father, Downs Foster, a carpenter who grew up on a farm at Fishing Creek, eventually became keeper of the Cape May Lighthouse and followed his own father's footsteps as a church trustee.

Reuben Foster chose another route in life after the war, relocating to Baltimore and becoming an official with York River Steamboat Company. He eventually incorporated his own outfit, the Chesapeake Steamship Company. Back home, Amelia Hand personally felt the pain of the 25th's experience at Fredericksburg. "In the last terrible sunset charge," she wrote in her diary, "among those that fell was my dear friend and future husband Edward Townsend." Wounded in the side by a musket ball, Sergeant Townsend at least had not been left on the battlefield. Carried back to a house, he held out for a day. He was buried in a garden near the battlefield. The couple was to be married at the end of Townsend's enlistment, the following summer.

Amelia counted back five generations of the Hand family in Cape May County, fourth of nine children of Franklin Hand, who'd married into the

Stillwell and Whildin families. As with many of those old-time connected families, the Hands sent several sons off to serve the Union cause.

Amelia's older brother David, a doctor in St. Paul, Minnesota, at the outbreak of hostilities, enlisted as an army surgeon after First Bull Run. He was placed in charge of the hospital at Newport News. But first he experienced the horrors of war firsthand with the Army of the Potomac during the Battles of Five Oaks and Seven Pines. He also served as medical director at Suffolk.

Amelia maintained a scrapbook. Intermixed with her own experiences at home during the war, her entries vary from describing Bull Run as a "bloody and desperate battle in which both armys [*sic*] thought themselves defeated and broke and fled in wild confusion" to discussing a "very pleasant winter in Philadelphia visiting Independence Hall and hearing Henry Ward Beecher preach." She also detailed the county's response to the first draft. After the township made its quota, Franklin Hand apparently caught war fever. He enlisted for three years in the 6th New Jersey Infantry Regiment. Amelia recorded heartbreak when news reached the county about Fredericksburg. "Our New Jersey 25th went into action and as will be remembered by some of us at Cape May with sorrow, was in the hottest of the conflict," she wrote. "Oh this horrid, this cruel war. How many hearts and homes 'tis desolating and yet we cannot see the end, the prospect looks darker than when it began."

She listed the dead and wounded from Cape May County. In addition to her Edward, Albert Edmunds was killed. Like Amelia Hand, Edmunds came from a long-established county family. His grandfather fought in the War of 1812. His father, Richard Downs Edmunds, was a Lower Township farmer and merchant who also served as county sheriff and freeholder before going to the state assembly in 1875.

Jeremiah Tyler was wounded and subsequently died. Joseph Hughes, William F. Smith, Daniel H. White, Samuel Hann, James Eldridge, Coleman F. Ludlam, John Hoffman, Richard German, Charles Mills, William Farrow and Alonzo Willett were all wounded. Joseph Garrison, James L. Grace, William Snyder, Morris V. Warren and Leaming Weatherby went missing and were presumed captured.

She added a more upbeat postscript to this somber roll call. "The 6th New Jersey, being used as reserves, suffered little. Consequently, my brother Franklin came off unhurt." But she recorded more deaths on December 21, this time from an even more lethal killer: disease. "Daniel Hildreth, Company I, died in camp of typhoid fever. And Maurice Stites, Company G died in regiment hospital from the same disease....Both were in the battleat Fredericksburg and came out unhurt only to fall victim to a disease that has proved fatal to so many of our brave soldiers."

Hildreth's grave is one of about fifty Civil War headstones located at Cape May Court House Baptist Cemetery. He died at age twenty-seven. His memorial, from his wife, reads, "Farewell my husband farewell/ For we shall meet no more/ til we are raised with thee to dwell on Zion's happier shore."

After its hot welcome to the realities of war, the 25th remained at Falmouth for a month. Joseph Holmes, writing to his mother on January 19, 1863, expressed satisfaction upon receiving his first "hand" (letter) since December. "We may stay here all winter. We know as much about what we are going to do as you do." He described preparing living quarters, sealing it with used "cracker boxes" for the winter. "The men occupy their evenings singing songs before the makeshift fireplace while daytime is devoted primarily to drilling."

Holmes announced his promotion to commissary sergeant. "We get pretty good rations now, getting fresh beef twice a week and beans, pork, sugar, coffee, rice. I have to see to drawing rations every day and dealing it out to the company."

The regiment enjoyed a visit from Dr. Gilman (Uriah), then serving as assistant surgeon for three years with the 12th New Jersey Infantry. "He wears a sword and rides the same horse he had while at Court House." Holmes entertained another Court House neighbor, Richard Swain Thompson, also of the 12th. Holmes completed his enlistment with the 25th and then reenlisted with the 3rd New Jersey Cavalry, achieving the rank of second lieutenant by May 1865.

Descended from vintage Cape May County stock, Holmes's roots extended to the Leaming and Hand families. His father, Richard Collins Holmes, was a judge in Cape May Court House, where he owned considerable land and a house where Joseph lived after the war. The house, as of this writing, serves as a museum for the County of Cape May.

Another letter writer in the regiment was Hollis Perry Mickel. The farm boy from Upper Township experienced picket duty along the Rappahannock after a quick encounter with Stonewall Jackson. "Our regiment went out on picket duty abreast of Fredericksburg," he wrote home on New Year's morning, 1863. "We could see plenty of rebels stirrin' in town....I was close enough to rebels to see and hear them talking as the river is quite narrow. I guess I could throw a stone across it into town. We was out in open sight but there was not a gun fired."

While Mickel enjoyed the new year with a meal of bean soup and hard tack, he visualized "feasting at home on spare rib." Instead of griping about cold weather, he expressed thanks that, unlike so many of his comrades, he hadn't gotten sick—"if we have our health here we can get along."

Five days later, Mickel described picket duty, "close enough to the rebels to talk to them. Two or three rebels came across the river and one of them gave us a Richmond paper and another come over and stayed—he said that Gen. Lee prayed all the time that we was in Fredericksburg to [attack] him again and the night we was in the engagement he said they did not open much more than half their batterys on us and all they wanted was for us to make another charge."

In early February, the regiment was transferred to Newport News. Leach recognized the steamer used to convey the troops. The *George Washington*, the reporter recalled, "carried as many as 560 passengers to Cape Island during summer season."

The 25th remained at Newport News until mid-March, when it headed to Suffolk. Dismal Swamp became its new home, guarding the rail line to Portsmouth. The aptly named swamp reflected the mood of the troops after the debacle at Fredericksburg.

Burnside was replaced by Hooker. As Granville Leach wrote, "The 25th still lives and the boys are jolly enough for now, having had a visit from a longed-for gentleman whom we know as Mr. Pay Master." He came bearing two months' soldier pay—in greenbacks.

Another countian from Company F, Jeremiah Tyler, succumbed in January at Newark hospital from wounds received in action.

Fellow Company F private Charles Riel survived Fredericksburg and completed his enlistment. However, Riel would suffer his entire life from medical ailments incurred during the Fredericksburg Campaign. Applying to increase his eight-dollar monthly pension at age seventy in 1905, Riel documented chronic diseases of stomach, bowels and urinary organs, as well as rheumatism, arising from contracting kidney disease and jaundice during his service. Riel's increase was approved to twelve dollars per month. He died less than two years later. The 25th joined the 3rd Division, designated to defend Suffolk. While awaiting an anticipated Rebel offensive, Leach reported another death: John Robinson, from Dennisville. Robinson caught a "severe chill while on night guard duty and by morning," according to the correspondent. "He was unconscious in his tent." The doctor diagnosed cause of death as "congestion of the brain."

Married with children, Robinson was, in Leach's words, "a true soldier. Kind and warm-hearted comrade…ever present, never angry and always endeavoring to do justly with all around him."

While the main Army of the Potomac fought an unsuccessful battle at Chancellorsville, the 25th participated in a smaller engagement at Suffolk. Quiet on that front was broken when the regiment entertained a few visitors, about thirty thousand—all wearing butternut. Their objective was to seize enemy supplies while threatening Portsmouth and Norfolk.

Longstreet's Confederates attacked over the course of several days until April 14, when Union gunboats joined the battle. The Rebels continued to press, bringing up reinforcements during the last week of April to confront the dug-in Union line. The 25th was ordered forward to ascertain enemy strength and disposition. The Jersey men were greeted by horrendous fire from the enemy.

The regiment formed a battle line. Under persistent fire, they gradually nudged the enemy out of its position. At one point, according to Leach, the regiment "formed a line in an open cornfield to fight the johnnies who skulked in the woods." Reinforcements joined their movement, and the battle was won with Rebel rifle pits falling into Union hands. Longstreet abandoned the siege.

When Company G's commander was wounded in the battle, Second Lieutenant Nicholas Corson from Upper Township assumed that role. Company G contained a number of Upper Township men.

Born in Seaville in 1833, Corson was a schoolteacher, according to the 1860 census. Like many men from Upper, he first joined the Seaville Rangers, under the command of fellow Upper resident Joseph Corson (no relation). The Seaville Rangers became a core component of Company G. The regiment's original captain was Joseph Powell, a blacksmith who resigned on December 22, 1862, following the Battle of Fredericksburg—coincidentally, or not, the same date on which Company F's David Blenkow (captain) and Nicholas Godfrey (lieutenant) also resigned.

Joseph Corson would return to the county after the war, becoming tax collector for a new municipality developed on the barrier islands in the postwar era, Ocean City. He held the post until 1909, when he died of "nervous disease" at age seventy-six.

Other county men were wounded in this engagement. Eldora resident John Chambers, Company F, received his second combat wound in less than a year, having also been wounded at Fredericksburg.

25th New Jersey Volunteers battle flag. *njmilitiamuseum.org.*

Private Clark Elliott was also wounded at Suffolk. Elliott survived the war. He operated a farm in Lower Township and would also serve on the governing body for Lower.

The regiment's next movement brought it near Norfolk. There, the men cast aside weapons of destruction for tools of construction. They built a fort, aptly named Fort New Jersey, which occupied five acres. This fort outlasted the Confederacy, a monument of sorts for the 25th.

All the while, according to Granville Leach, the regiment operated warily, being in "unfriendly territory." "There is scarce a house held in this vicinity that has not parted with one or more male members who are in the confederate army," Leach reported. "It is needless to say the people sympathize with the south."

But their nine months living in hostile country soon drew to a close. The regiment was ordered out to Portsmouth on June 4. Its term of service completed, the 25th returned to Beverly on June 6 and later that month was officially mustered out on June 20, 1863.

A former commander wrote of the nine-month men, "They improved as soldiers with great rapidity from the most inexperienced, they have become worthy to be ranked as veterans…they return home with the proud consciousness of having done their duty."

Some members of the 25th returned to combat, joining other New Jersey regiments. Jonathan Cliver, a private in the 25th, reenlisted with the 2nd Volunteer Cavalry. He served in the western theater from September 1864 until June 1865 and was discharged at Vicksburg.

One thousand men left New Jersey under the aegis of the 25th Infantry regiment. Fewer than seven hundred returned. "The bones of some are now bleaching on the sun-scorched battlefields of Virginia," Leach wrote. "The remains of others rest beneath the sod in some desolate soldier's grave and on a distant southern hillside."

Leach's final dispatch for the 25th appeared in the paper's July 2 edition, while more blood and tears were being shed on a farm field in a place called Gettysburg.

3RD CAVALRY

The Civil War wasn't the only thing on the minds of readers of the *Ocean Wave* at the beginning of 1864. Real estate was selling along the intended route of the progressing railroad. The paper advertised lots for sale in and around Woodbine by William Townsend, who owned much land in that area. Eventually, a town named Belleplain developed, named honoring the "most beautiful woman in Cape May County," who happened to be Townsend's daughter. A beauty that was the stuff of legend, Annabel Townsend, some claimed, inspired one of Poe's last poems, "Annabel Lee."

The county was again enrolling men to fill its quota. Nine-month veterans from the 25th Infantry mustered out the summer before reenlisted, this time joining the cavalry. Instead of nine-month hitches, they signed for three years or war's duration.

Meeting quotas and avoiding drafts caused concern for the county since its inception. New Jersey governor Parker announced that no draft had yet been ordered for the state, as "thirty days were allowed to raise sufficient volunteers." Cape May County had its work cut out.

The *Ocean Wave* offered better news. Prospects for the "season" at Cape Island pointed to a "rich summer." "Now that the Rebs have been defeated in their invasion of the north [Gettysburg] and the weather has become warm." The paper anticipated an extended season into September, "instead of breaking up in August as heretofore."

But there was still a war to be won, and men were needed to fight it. The county struggled to raise troops and appeared likely to rely on the "revolving draft wheel." By mid-December, it was the "prevailing topic of conversation."

The paper concluded that there was only one solution: pay men to "volunteer" like other counties were doing. But who would pay? The well-to-do? The townships? The county? The paper pointed to the county while encouraging those financially situated to contribute to the county's "bounty fund."

Joseph Holmes of Cape May Court House was commissioned an officer in the 3rd Cavalry. The paper trumpeted the announcement to encourage others to sign up. Alfred Cooper, longtime publisher of the *Cape May County Gazette*, remembered Holmes. Cooper's mother was "heavily involved in civic matters," he wrote years later in his memoir. "During the Civil War, she was a leader in sewing and picking lint [for bandages] for the soldiers. And in the day of no railroad below Millville, the women of that town always fed the troops from Cape May County on their way to be mustered in….Joseph Holmes used to speak to me about 'those breakfasts those Millville women served before we went to war.'"

Holmes enjoyed the hospitality of Millville on two occasions apparently, first when he joined 25th Infantry and when he reenlisted with the 3rd Cavalry.

The *Ocean Wave* continued calling for volunteers in its December 12 edition. "The famished carcass of the rebel army is on its last legs," the editor frothed, suggesting that war-weary Southerners were "making overtures to return to their allegiance." The final push required more men to do the pushing. "Now's the time to join. Big Bounty. Good pay. A scrimmage or two in which to smell the powder and become a hero. The war ended and a safe return home."

The county got the ball rolling that week by forming a committee, which prepared a resolution for county freeholders urging that body to institute a $500 bounty per recruit. Prominent locals including Dr. Coleman Leaming, Franklin Hand, Stephen H. Bennett, John Ross, Douglass, Sumner Marcy and William Garrison solicited enlistments.

Captain John Franklin Tomlin, about to serve in the 3rd Cavalry, encouraged recruits. Tomlin was "a man of known integrity who has smelled the powder while in the nine-month regiment," the paper assured readers. Tomlin was further lauded for his "coolness under fire, giving his orders with the spirit and decision of a veteran." The county's boys would be in good hands.

The paper's first 1864 edition noted the "lively interest taken in rousing recruits to fill the county quota." Freeholders appointed another committee to oversee enlistments for individual townships. Thomas Williams (Upper),

Clinton Ludlam (Dennis), Leaming (Middle), Miller (Lower) and George Smith (formerly of the 7th) were selected. Coleman Leaming handled the purse, disbursing the money. The county's Black population also stepped up, with many of them enlisting.

George Smith left Cape Island with five men. Charles Shaw followed next day with five more. Lower topped both, sending fifteen men. With few days remaining, Captain Tomlin was successful "recruiting Hussars, primarily in Dennis and Upper Townships."

Recruits came from assorted work backgrounds. Farmers and construction laborers mostly, but the regiment also boasted blacksmiths, sailors, brewers, painters, butchers, bakers and, yes, a candlestick maker. The ranks even included a professional actor.

Cape Island Council sweetened the bounty pot, adding fifty dollars for each volunteer, while a "private bounty" chipped in another five dollars per man. "Cape May County," the *Ocean Wave* boasted, "had offered the highest bounty in the state."

The 3rd New Jersey Cavalry, drawing many of these volunteers, comprised the state's newest regiment, New Jersey's 36th. It consisted of 1,200 enlisted men and officers. Headquartered at Camp Bayard in Trenton, the regiment was designated U.S. Hussars. What was a hussar? Unlike "dragoons," the original intent of the hussar unit was to serve as light cavalry. Typically, they rode smaller, faster horses suitable for scouting and messenger duty.

Initially armed with sabers and pistols, the 3rd eventually fully armed with rifles as the regiment engaged in combat.

The paper noted the regiment's departure in its April 7 edition. "Twelve hundred strong and fully equipped, they left for the front after meeting the governor." Their distinctive uniforms made them easily recognizable when they joined the Army of the Potomac cavalry corps at Alexandria.

The newcomers from New Jersey caught some razzing from grizzled front-line veterans. Those uniforms didn't help. The uniforms modeled those worn by hussars in Austria. Instead of overcoats worn by other regiments, the 3rd sported "talmas," large cloaks with tassels stylishly displayed over the left shoulder. Their headgear took the unusual form of "pillbox" cap with a soft top. The cap, bearing the number "3" within a wreath, was trimmed with yellow cord. "The seams and edges of their jackets are trimmed with yellow lace, the breast is ornamented with parallel stripes of the same material running crosswise about an inch apart with loops at the sides and centers surrounding brass buttons," wrote a Michigan cavalryman familiar with the 3rd. Jeering detractors called them "butterflies."

Private Daniel Wheaton of the 3rd New Jersey is buried at Calvary Baptist Cemetery in Ocean View. *www.findagrave.com.*

The highest-ranking officer in the 3rd from the county was Second Lieutenant John Franklin Tomlin, elder brother to Andrew. Born in 1840, the Goshen native had held a lieutenant's rank in the 25th. With the 3rd, Tomlin commanded Company E.

Holmes, another alumnus of the 25th, mustered in with the 3rd as a sergeant. He'd be promoted to second lieutenant in May 1865 and remained with the cavalry until August of that year.

Money was an incentive to enlist, but the paper noted that with the war's end "not far off…the strong probability is that men now being called into service will not be required for the full term [three years]."

Typical of those enlisting with an appreciation of those bounties was Corporal Daniel Wheaton. Writing to his brother, Willets, from Trenton, Wheaton expressed anxiousness to move out, having been "in camp nearly three weeks. I want to get out and buy a few notions I need."

Then he discussed bounty money. "The bounty from the county is $300.…We get $65 now in cash. I am going to have $30 brought to me and the rest I will leave for father to collect at Coleman Leaming's. The [federal] government bounty I suppose we will get in installments."

The April 14 *Ocean Wave* listed new enlistees by race and township, starting with Lewis Gooden from Cape Island and John Wiley Hand from Lower.

The 3rd initially posted in Virginia, three miles south of Bristow Station, along the Orange and Alexandria Railroad. It performed scouting and guard duty along the Rapidan River during the Battle of the Wilderness. Two companies were detached for orderly duty, while another was sent to Fredericksburg to police the town and establish a hospital to receive casualties from the ongoing battle.

According to John Young Foster, "every church, store, and other commodious building was occupied…crowded with sufferers…rows of dead were found lying in dilapidated outhouses and night and day, stretchers with dead and dying drifted along the streets."

For veterans of the 25th now serving in the 3rd, memories were powerful and painful. The corduroy roads, swampy overgrown terrain…Fredericksburg. Instead of a futile charge against a well-defended position, the 3rd was held out of front-line action, battle sounds heard at a distance. "I cannot tell you where I am, only that I am in Virginia between Fredericksburg to Richmond," Corporal Thomas H. Taylor from Cape May wrote home. "We are trying to work our way to Richmond but it is very slow."

Another county man present during this campaign was Private Lewis Gooden. Gooden was actually born in Harlem but came to Cape Island as an infant to live with relatives after his mother suddenly died. A member of Company A, Gooden fought at Cold Harbor and Petersburg. Serving as a dispatch rider for General Ambrose Burnside, he was wounded in the leg near the end of the war. After his discharge, Gooden joined other county residents headed west. He lived in Illinois and Nebraska before marrying and settling down in Indiana.

Another veteran of the 3rd who went west after the war was Private Francis Gurney Springer. He migrated to Illinois, before putting down roots in Kansas.

Greeting card depicting 3rd Cavalry trooper from Tradition Studios, Woodstock, Virginia. *Postcard collection, Dennis Township Old School House Museum.*

On August 5, Grant transferred the 3rd to the Shenandoah Valley, joining the cavalry corps commanded by General Phillip Sheridan. Many Union generals believed that cavalry's role should be limited to guard or picket details while infantry and artillery performed the heavy lifting of actual combat. Sheridan took a more aggressive view. He wanted horse soldiers in the thick of battle. And he had the ear of the one man empowered to give him the go-ahead. Grant's order was typically direct: "Concentrate your available mounted forces and proceed against the enemy's cavalry"—exactly what Sheridan wanted to hear.

Henceforth, the 3rd had three goals: disrupt Rebel supplies and railroads, threaten the enemy capital and defeat opposition cavalry. They busied themselves with the first objective, destroying locomotives, cars, wagons and eight miles of track and telegraph lines. In the process, they captured tons of medical supplies and rations meant for Lee's needy army.

The regiment suffered a serious setback when setting out to destroy a branch of the Virginia Central Railroad. Routed and in retreat, about forty members of the 3rd were captured. These men were sent to Confederate prison camps. Among those taken were county men Shamgar Townsend and Alfred Warwick.

Corporal Townsend was sent to Andersonville and Private Warwick to Salisbury. Townsend survived his captivity, was paroled and was discharged to U.S. Army General Hospital in York, Pennsylvania, on May 12. Warwick, from Company A, fourth of eight children of a Court House farmer, was eighteen years old when he died of starvation on October 6, 1864. He was buried at Poplar Grove National Cemetery in Virginia. That same year, his twenty-four-year-old brother, Amos, died in a shipwreck near Fort Monroe.

Originally a textile mill, Salisbury was the only prison in North Carolina. By the time of Warwick's stay, the facility, intended to hold 2,500 prisoners, held more than 10,000. Many were Union troops captured during the protracted siege of Richmond.

Poor sanitation and lack of food were chronic problems. Correspondingly, health problems proliferated, particularly diarrhea. More than 25 percent of Salisbury's prisoners died in the waning days of the war. Bodies were carted to hastily dug trenches and thrown in.

Andersonville was worse. Andersonville's inmates were quartered outdoors. According to the *New Jersey Herald*, men's "lips were parched and cracked and bleeding, wild glaring eyes started from their heads and all the while they gibbered half intelligibly and scrambled like wild beasts for the smallest crumbs thrown to them."

About 240 New Jersey prisoners, 7 of them Hussars, died at Andersonville. According to Peter Lubrecht's *New Jersey Butterfly Boys in the Civil War*, another 11 Jersey men were buried at Salisbury; 27 men from the 3rd were imprisoned at Salisbury. Some of those who were freed later died from medical complications arising from their imprisonment.

The end of 1964 brought more sad news for the Cape May County men of the 3rd. Private James McGill, Company G, a Tuckahoe glass blower, died on December 28 of chronic diarrhea (dysentery) at Mower Army General Hospital in Philadelphia.

Down to about four hundred actives, the 3rd's firepower improved when the men were armed with brand-new Spencer repeating carbines (seven shots with one loading), which they soon put to use.

The regiment fought at Winchester on August 17. Placed in support of two artillery batteries on a hilltop at an advanced skirmish line, the men fought Tennessee Rebels at close quarters well into the night, taking heavy casualties—130 killed, wounded or captured. Sheridan noted the "gallant charge" of the 3rd Regiment that included capture of an entire South Carolina regiment.

For troop movements on September 12, the 3rd was dispatched to the Berryville and Winchester Pike on a scouting mission, intelligence from which helped Sheridan plan his next move. Encountering Rebel cavalry, the regiment chased them until they reached infantry fortifications at Berryville. The 3rd forced the issue, taking 143 prisoners.

Contending armies next positioned for what would be a decisive battle on September 19, again at Winchester. The 3rd was involved from the outset, driving enemy cavalry down Winchester Pike, reaching Karneystown, Front Royal and up Luray Valley before withdrawing.

By nightfall, they had joined a massive Union cavalry charge against Jubal Early's army. Action was close, with men compelled to dismount to work their repeating rifles. Casualties mounted on both sides. Union losses in the victory exceeded four thousand killed or wounded.

The Battle of Winchester was auspicious for another reason. The 3rd was assigned a new commanding officer: George Armstrong Custer. The flamboyant Custer was known for the red scarf he wore around his neck. Men of the 3rd adopted the practice as a show of affection for their twenty-three-year-old leader.

Custer led the regiment on several successful skirmishes. Grant, determined to be rid of Mosby's raiders, ordered Sheridan's cavalry to "destroy or carry off crops, animals, Negroes, and all men under 50 capable of bearing arms" in the Shenandoah Valley. They did so with such vigor that more than $3 million damage was done before they were through.

October 19, 1864, was a date that would become famous. It was the day Sheridan made his famous "ride," rallying his troops, turning certain rout into major victory. According to Peter Lubrecht, it was the "battle that saved the election," winning the presidency in 1864 for Abraham Lincoln.

Winter passed quietly as the regiment prepared for its final campaign in February 1865.

Heavy rain complicated the 3rd's movements as it crossed a flooded creek, with some currents carrying men off. And waiting on the other side—not with hot coffee and warm blankets—were Rebels in force. The 3rd attacked the flank, pushing forward into Waynesboro where it again encountered opposition, positioned behind earthworks. This time, the Rebels had artillery.

The regiment dismounted and penetrated the Rebel line through a gap in a heavily wooded area. The Yanks routed and chased them for miles. The result opened the Blue Ridge Mountains for the Union. Demoralized Confederates lost valuable supplies and artillery, along with 1,800 men taken prisoner, according to Custer's report of the battle. The 3rd suffered no casualties. Not only the momentum but also the attitude of the local population shifted in favor of the Union.

By the end of March, Sheridan's army was moving toward Petersburg, where a dismounted 3rd fought W.H.F. Lee's cavalry near Dinwiddie Court House. After days of give and take fighting, Lee retreated, a rout Lubrecht termed the Confederate "Waterloo." The Battle of Five Forks marked the beginning of the end for Rebel forces in Virginia.

According to the *New York Times*, as Custer rode at the head of his column, men sprang to the roadside cheering, "There's the fella who flanked the Rebs at Five Forks!"

Among the names reported in the paper as wounded during the battle was "JF Tomlin, Company M, 3rd NJ." Tomlin would recover from his wound.

In addition to generals, Federals took an estimated ten thousand disheartened prisoners as the Army of Northern Virginia rapidly disintegrated. Facing imminent defeat, the enemy abandoned battle flags, artillery, hundreds of horses, arms and ammunition and "six miles of wagon trains."

By April 8, Custer was leading his men toward Appomattox Station, driving back discouraged Southerners. The next day, Custer sent a message to his regiment from Appomattox Court House, congratulating them for their success in a just concluded war. "When those deeds of daring," wrote Custer, "which have rendered the name and fame of the 3rd Cavalry imperishable, are inscribed upon the bright pages of our country's history, I only ask that my name be written as that of Commander of the 3rd Cavalry Division."

History would record Custer's name larger in connection with another cavalry battle at another time and place.

AFTER

fter the war, Henry Sawyer returned to a hero's welcome, a medal and a parade. Then he went to work. Another Sawyer brother-in-law, Francis K. Duke, a southerner by birth (Harper's Ferry, Virginia), relocated to the county before the war, married Sophia Louise Eldredge (1853) and became a successful builder. Duke fought for the Union, enlisting in Delaware's 2nd Regiment in 1861. He fought all the engagements around Richmond. Duke suffered a broken leg at Fair Oaks when a bullet pierced the limb. His neck was wounded at Savage Station—he'd just been promoted to captain. After the war, he flourished as a builder. Among his larger projects was the Peermont Hotel in Avalon, a new resort on a heretofore undeveloped barrier island north of Cape May. Built in 1889, the Peermont was a three-story wooden structure with tall widow's peaks and wraparound porch. Duke completed the job in less than two months.

In order to enhance the new hotel's status, he brought in a big-name manager to run it: brother-in-law Sawyer. Like Sawyer, Duke engaged in local politics, serving as justice of the peace and coroner, and joined Sawyer on Cape May's City Council.

In 1867, Henry Sawyer—carpenter, cavalryman and POW—became a Cape Island hotelier. He assumed ownership of the Ocean House, operating it for six years before relocating to Wilmington to manage Clayton House, at five stories and 105 rooms the premier hotel in that city.

But Sawyer had sand in his shoes. He returned to Cape Island. In 1872, he bought land on Sewell Avenue and built the eighteen-room Chalfonte Hotel.

Scars of war healed, and wealthy southerners returned to the cape during summer months. Sawyer's hotel became a favorite stop. Its kitchen was renowned for southern cuisine. "After the war, where once blood flowed, flowers now grow," Sawyer was quoted as saying. "We are one people again, greatest country of the world....All is forgiven."

He doubled the size of his Chalfonte two years later, adding a cupola from which he could look out over his town. One night, in 1878, Sawyer observed smoke pouring from the roof of Ocean House on Washington Street. Sawyer sounded the alarm, but it was too late. A major fire destroyed thirty-five acres, much of the old construction in the resort, but Sawyer's Chalfonte was spared. The fire of 1878 reduced Cape May's available rooms by 90 percent. It also marked the end of the era of building jumbo hotels like the Mount Vernon. Sawyer remained at the helm of Chalfonte until he sold it in 1888.

In addition to the hotel business, Sawyer served on Cape May City Council for several terms. He later took another government post, superintendent of U.S. Life-Saving Service for coastal New Jersey. That post would increase in importance as the county developed its barrier islands. This service eventually became the U.S. Coast Guard.

Sawyer remained prominent and very visible in Cape May. Seen riding about town on a white stallion, his "trademark," Sawyer's renown was such that when John Philip Sousa's band performed at Congress Hall in 1882, Sawyer introduced him to the audience.

During his twilight years, Sawyer came full circle. In 1889, Harriet died. Having sold the Chalfonte in 1888, Sawyer returned to farm life on ninety-two acres he'd purchased offshore. He grew vegetables, which he sold to resort

Opposite: Peermont Hotel in Avalon was built by a Civil War veteran and first managed by a Civil War veteran. *Avalon Historical Museum.*

This page, top: Postcard promoting Sawyer's Chalfonte Hotel. *Cape May County Museum.*

This page, bottom: Artist's rendering of 1876 fire that destroyed much of "old" Cape May. *National Park Service.*

hotels. He lived "quietly" with his second wife, Mary Emma McKissick, a schoolteacher he met while managing Hotel Peermont.

He maintained a public presence with personal appearances. A December 1881 *Cape May Wave* reported on Sawyer's lecture at the South Dennis Methodist Church. While his topic was the war service of the recently assassinated President (and former general) James Garfield, the audience insisted on hearing about his Libby Prison experiences. "The colonel's audience was large and attentive…his lecture so full of eloquence and power from a *live* colonel of the late war of rebellion."

Sawyer maintained his Civil War connection until his death in 1893. According to his obituary, he "dropped dead of heart failure on the floor in Marcy and Mecray's drug store." He'd gone there to order a "special type of soda for aiding digestion." Muffled drum rolls and bugle call taps accompanied the many veterans escorting his remains to Cold Spring Cemetery. His funeral procession, according to the paper, was "a mile long, the largest ever known at this end of the state."

Bibliography

Books

Bilby, Joseph. *Freedom for All: New Jersey's African-American Civil War Soldiers.* Hightstown, NJ: Longstreet House, 2011.

———. *New Jersey Civil War Odyssey.* New Jersey: New Jersey Civil War Heritage Association Sesquicentennial, 2011.

Billings, John David. *Hardtack and Coffee: The Unwritten Story of Army Life.* Chicago: Lakeside Press, 1960.

Biographical Genealogical, and Descriptive History of the 1ˢᵗ Congressional District of New Jersey. Vols 1–2. Chicago: Lewis Publishing Company.

Champion, Thomas, and Raymond Rebmann. *Dennis Township.* Charleston, SC: Arcadia Publishing, 2016.

Clinton, Catherine. *Harriet Tubman: The Road to Freedom.* New York: Little, Brown and Company, 2005.

Cooper, Alfred. *My Traditions and Memories, 1859–1938.* Cape May Court House, NJ: Gazette Print Shop, 1938.

Cornish, Dudley. *The Sable Army.* New York: W.W. Norton & Company, 1966.

Craig, Stanley. *History of Petersburg, New Jersey.* Merchantville, NJ: H. Stanley Craig, 1913.

Cunningham, John. *New Jersey: America's Main Road.* New York: Doubleday, 1966.

Dobak, William. *Freedom by the Sword: Official Army History of the U.S. Colored Troops in the Civil War.* Washington, D.C.: U.S. Army Center of Military History, 2013.

Dorwart, Jeffrey. *Cape May County, New Jersey.* New Brunswick, NJ: Rutgers University Press, 1992.

Foster, John Young. *New Jersey and the Rebellion.* New York: Franklin Classics, 1996.

Francine, Albert Phillip, AM, MD. *Louis Raymond Francine, Brevet Brigadier U.S. Volunteers.* Hightstown, NJ: Longstreet House, 2000.

Godfrey, Carlos. *Sketch of Major HW Sawyer*. Trenton, NJ: MacCrellish and Quigley, 1907.

Gragg, Rod. *Confederate Goliath: Battle of Fort Fisher*. New York: HarperCollins, 2006.

———. *Eyewitness Gettysburg*. New York: Regnery History, 2016.

Hand, Albert. *A Book of Cape May, New Jersey*. Cape May Court House, NJ: Albert Hand Company, 1937.

Hayward, John. *Give It to Them: Jersey Blues*. Hightstown, NJ: Longstreet House, 1998.

Hennessy, Mary. *His Hour Upon the Stage*. New York: Vantage Press, 2007.

Holden, Robert. *Upper Township and Its Ten Villages*. Charleston, SC: Arcadia Publishing, 2020.

Jackson, William. *New Jerseyans in the Civil War*. New Brunswick, NJ: Rivergate Books, 2000.

Jago, Frederick. *12ᵗʰNew Jersey Volunteers, 1862–65*. Woodbury, NJ: Gloucester County Historical Society, 1967.

Kenny, Kevin. *Making Sense of the Molly Maguires*. New York: Oxford University Press, 1998.

Lee, Jorena. *The Life and Religious Experience of Jorena Lee*. N.p., 1836.

Longacre, Edward. *The Sharpshooters*. Hightstown, NJ: Longstreet House, 2017.

———. *To Gettysburg and Beyond*. Hightstown, NJ: Longstreet House, 1988.

Lubrecht, Peter. *New Jersey Butterfly Boys in the Civil War*. Charleston, SC: The History Press, 2011.

An Oral History of Somers Corson. Barbara Horan and Lynn Dress, interviewers. Tuckahoe, NJ: Upper Township Historical Society, 2012.

Porris, Gerry, and Ralf Porris. *While My Country Is in Danger*. Hamilton, NY: Edmonston Publishing, 1994.

Potter, David. *The Impending Crisis: America Before the Civil War*. New York: Harper Perennial, 1976.

Remember You Are Jersey Men. Hightstown, NJ: Longstreet House, 2011.

Rizzo, Dennis. *Parallel Communities: Underground Railroad in South Jersey*. Charleston, SC: The History Press, 2008.

Robinson, Charles M., III. *Hurricane of Fire*. Annapolis, MD: Naval Institute Press, 1998.

Siebert, Wilbur. *Underground from Slavery to Freedom*. Newburyport, MA: Amed Literary, 2006.

Siegel, Alan. *Beneath the Starry Flag*. New Brunswick, NJ: Rutgers University Press, 2001.

Stevens, Lewis Townsend. *History of Cape May County*. Alpha Editions. Originally published in 1897.

Still, William. *The Underground Railroad Records*. London: Vintage, 2000.

Switala, William. *Underground Railroad in New York and New Jersey*. Mechanicsburg, PA: Stackpole Books, 2006.

Tomlin, Charles. *Cape May Spray*. N.p.: Bradley Brothers, 1913.

Toombs, Samuel. *New Jersey Troops in the Gettysburg Campaign*. Hightstown, NJ: Big Byte Books, 1988.

Watson, Bill. *The Ludlam Legacy*. Stroudsburg, PA: Broken Lance Enterprises, 2011.

Weiss, Harry. *Life in Early New Jersey*. New York: D. Van Nordstrand, 1964.

Wittenberg, Eric, and Davis Daniel. *Out Flew the Sabres*. El Dorado Hills, CA: Savas Beatie, 2016.

Articles and Papers

Barrat, Norris. "Josiah Granville Leach." *Journal of Pennsylvania State University*. 2015.

Barton, Christopher P. "Antebellum African-American Settlements in Southern New Jersey." African Diaspora Archaeology Network, December 2009. University of Massachusetts–Amherst.

Campbell, Jim. "My Dear Wife—A Letter from a Soldier." *Newsletter of Cape May Historical Society* (2001).

Coddington, Ron. "Defending Bliss Barn." *Civil War News* (July 2013).

Dalton, Peter. "Percy, Old Boy!" *Shenandoah Valley's Civil War* (blog). www. shenandoahcivilwarhistory.blog.

Dreyfuss, Barbara. "Freedom's Corner." *Cape May Magazine* (2019).

———. "Stephen Smith, Cape May Underground Railroad Leader." *Cape May Magazine* (2015).

Dreyfuss, Barbara, and James Terbush. "Cape May Connection." *Cape May Magazine* (2021).

Edmiston, Samantha. "Molly Maguireism and Unionism During the Civil War." Thesis, Old Dominion University, 2017. www.digitalcommons.odu.edu.

Elwell, Robert, Sr. "Another Civil War Hero." *Cape May Star and Wave* (2011).

Gregory, C.E. "Sketch of Major Henry W. Sawyer." New Jersey Adjutant General's Office, 1945.

Hartwig, D. Scott. "Unwilling Witness to the Rage at Gettysburg." National Park History, 2004. www.npshistory.com.

Henderson, Steward. "Role of the USCT in the American Civil War." *Battlefield Trust* (2020).

Kopp, Jennifer Brownstone. "A Feeling of Community Revisited, Cape-Island African American Heritage." *Cape May Magazine* (2015).

———. "Past Tense: Exploring a Former Cape May House with a History." *Cape May Magazine* (2000).

McReady, Blake. "The Fight for Historic Memory: Fort William Penn." *Journal of the Civil War Era* (2016).

Moore, William. "Early Negro Settlers of Cape May County." *Cape May County Historical and Genealogical Society* (1947).

Ohls, Gary. "Fort Fisher—Amphibious Victory in Civil War." U.S. Naval War College, 2006.

Powels, James. "Libby Prison: Lottery of Death." Warfare History Network, reprinted from *Civil War Quarterly* (2014).

Scheuch-Evans, Lewis. "Sir Percy Wyndham: American Civil War Union Army's Flamboyant English Cavalry Commander." *Military History Magazine* (2005).

Thompson, Richard S. "A Scrap at Gettysburg." Article dated February 11, 1897.

Van Voorst, Joyce. "Tales and Legends of Upper Township and Its Villages." *South Jersey Magazine* (1987).

Wittenberg, Eric. "Bvt. Lt. Col. Henry Washington Sawyer." Rantings of a Civil War Historian, 2009. www.civilwarcavalry.com.

———. "Colonel Henry Sawyer and the Chalfonte Hotel." Civil War Talk. www. civilwartalk.com/threads/colonel-Henry-Sawyer-and-the-Chalfonte-Hotel.

———. "Lives on the Line." *Civil War Times* (2017).

Zombek, Angela. "Libby Prison." Encyclopedia Virginia. www.encyclopedia virginia.org.

Websites

Asbell, Samuel. The Lost Black Legion. http://westjerseyhistory.org/LBL/site. shtml.

Bussanich, Leonard. "To Reach Sweet Home Again: The Impact of Soldiering on New Jersey's Troops During the American Civil War." New Jersey History. https://njh.libraries.rutgers.edu/index.php/njh.

Find a Grave. www.findagrave.com.

State of New Jersey Department of State. "Civil War Service Records, 1861–1865." https://wwwnet-dos.state.nj.us.

Warfare History Network. www.warfarehistorynetwork.com.

World History Project. "Second Battle of Fort Fisher." www.world history project.com.

Zbick, Jim. "Pennsylvania's Perfect Hell." America's Civil War, 1992. www. historynet.com.

Documents and Collections

The American Civil War. "Libby Prisoner of War Camp." 2017. www.mycivilwar. com/pow.va-libby.

Cape Fear Living History Society. "9th New Jersey Volunteer Regiment." www.cflhs. com.

Cape May County Historical and Genealogical Society. *Cape May County Magazine of History and Genealogy* (1930–present).

Cape May County Library. *Cape May County Ocean Wave* newspapers from the microfilm collection on file.

Cape May County Museum. "Remembrances of Company B 10th NJ Volunteers." Unpublished journal, William Heisler Donnelly.

Civil War Index. "12th New Jersey Infantry." www.civilwarindex.com/armynj/12th_ nj_infantry.

Dalton, Kyle. "The Direct and Logical Consequence—Germ Theory in the Civil War." National Museum of Civil War Medicine, October 8, 2020. www. civilwarmed.org.

Dennis Township Old School House Museum. Civil War Pension Records, Charles Riel.

Department of Military and Veterans Affairs, State of New Jersey. "Twenty-Second United States Colored Infantry." www.nj.gov/military/historyassets/documents.

Horan, Barbara. "Richard Somers Townsend, 1839–1925." Upper Township Historical Society.

Mahr, Michael. "Typhoid Fever, One of the Civil War's Deadliest Diseases." National Museum of Civil War Medicine, 2021. www.civilwarmed.org.

National Park Service. "Prelude to Gettysburg: The Battle of Brandy Station." www.nps.gov/get.blogs.prelude-to-Gettysburg-the battle-of-brandy-station.

The 12th New Jersey Regimental History. www.12thnjvolunteerscok.org.

Wiley Letters. "To the Independent Voters of Cape May." Cape May County Historical Society, 1846.

Williams, Rachel. "U.S. Sanitary and Christian Commissions and the Union War Effort." National Museum of Civil War Medicine, May 25, 2017. www.civilwarmed.org.

About the Author

Raymond Rebmann, retired after thirty years with the New Jersey Department of Labor, now works as a curator for the Old School House Museum in Dennisville, New Jersey. A reporter and columnist for twenty years for the *Cape May County Herald* newspaper, he has also authored several books, including *Prohibition in Cape May County* (The History Press), *Dennis Township* (Arcadia Publishing), *How Can You Give Up that Adorable Puppy* (Unlimited Publishing) and *Jersey Devil, Cursed Unfortunate* (MuseItUp). With his children grown and moved on, he lives in a log cabin in the woods of South Seaville with his wife, dog, cat and horse. In addition to writing, beachcombing and gardening, he is a determined home brewer with an experimental bent.